Free From Corporate America

A Tactical Guide to Success on Your Own Terms

By Jon Reed

Foreword By Rachel Meyers

FreeFromCorporateAmerica.com

Published by eCruiting Alternatives, Inc.
Web site: FreeFromCorporateAmerica.com

ISBN: 978-0-9725988-5-9
Available retail from Amazon.com
Available wholesale from Ingram and Baker & Taylor

Copy Edit by Emil Marx
Content Edit by Morris Rosenthal
Content Edit by Jennifer Gabrielle
Content Edit by Rachel Meyers
Interior Design by Jon Reed
Interior Design Consult and Proof by Sophie Delano
Initial Caricature Photo by Andrea Burns
Cover Design and Bio Caricature by Rusty Johnson
Web Site Research and Content Development by Jennifer Gabrielle
Web Site Design by Bronwen Hodgkinson of CDE Vision
Foreword by Rachel Meyers

Also by Jon Reed

The SAP Consultant Handbook (2002, samples at JonERP.com)
Resumes From Hell (2004, samples at ResumesFromHell.com)

Dedications

This book could not have been written without the support and counsel of my friend Naomi of Graychase.com. You have done the heavy lifting.

This book is also dedicated to Lynda – no matter where you are, you make me want to shine.

Rachel Meyers, co-author of *Resumes From Hell*, remains the best editor (and friend) a guy could ever have.

Most of this book was written at the Northampton Brewery (NorthamptonBrewery.com), a business that has thrived outside the corporate world for more than twenty years. I'd like to thank the current and former staff of the Brewery for putting up with me on the one hand, and providing me with indispensable comradery on the other.

During the year after 9/11, no one in my industry wanted to pay me on anything but incentives – except Andy Klee of Klee Associates, a bootstrap entrepreneur who left the corporate world and built a business from western Colorado. Andy put his belief in me where it counts: paid work in a rough economy. I would not have been able to finance this book without him.

Acknowledgements

Beyond those formally credited, many individuals were important to the development and realization of this book – too many to mention here. Apologies to anyone I have overlooked. Thanks to Will Katz, Sarah Larson, Cheryl Cave, Corrie Greathouse, Hayley Mermelstein, Deliah Rosel, Amy Zuckerman, Brian Trout, The Sullivan Family, Hidden-Tech members, the Hidden-Tech Board, Justin Lavelle, Rusty and Caroline Johnson, the SAP Mentor Community, and my mother for her belief in this project. Morris Rosenthal of Fonerbooks.com remains an indispensable colleague.

Thanks also goes out to Jennifer Gabrielle for a gutsy early edit of the manuscript. Sophie Delano did brilliant work on the book's interior when it was needed the most. Many published authors had an influence on my book – my thanks go out to them, and you can read more about their work on the FreeFromCorporateAmerica.com Web site in the "Resources" section. Finally, thanks to the inimitable Caron Bryan for applying some momentum to the final stages of this project. A formal shoutout to the Booker T. Washington Class of 1986 is also in order.

How This Book Relates to a Changing Economy

This book was written over the course of a three-year period from 2005 to 2008. Recent economic developments and social media trends have raised new questions about how the tactics in this book apply to a changing economy. The final chapter, "So You've Read The Book – Now What's Next?" explains how to get bonus material on this topic and join in the conversation.

Contents

Part VIII: Conclusion

"Jon wants us to learn from the mistakes he and others have made along the way: debt he acquired for the wrong reasons, feeling a sense of ownership of businesses he did not own, and back-burnering dreams for too long."

Book Foreword by Rachel Meyers

If you want to be told "Do what you love and the money will follow," put this book down immediately. Building a life that integrates passion and financial intelligence requires unflinching honesty, tough choices, and a creative approach to your career. Dogged belief in a simplistic motto won't get you there.

What follows is *Free From Corporate America*, Jon Reed's tactical guide to moving beyond dependence on the corporate world. One way to think of this book is as a life preserver for 9 to 5ers in peril.

So why are 9 to 5ers in peril? Because as Jon and others have noted, "the corporate contract is broken." The new reality of the American worker is that pension funds are shaky, jobs are being outsourced overseas, and "the company" no longer has our best interests in mind. We are all "free agents," and it's time we start behaving accordingly.

Conventional wisdom is that we're too busy working to achieve financial freedom and pursue our dreams. But if you're beholden to a paycheck, every last ounce of time and energy will be spent trying to please your boss, make ends meet, or both. Days will turn into months, months will turn into years, and you'll turn into a different person than you wanted to be.

Many people accept that tradeoff because they assume that retirement will afford them the opportunity to pursue their interests, whether it's to write a novel, travel to exotic places, or learn to speak Spanish. But what if you haven't saved enough to retire comfortably? What if you aren't healthy when you get there? And what are we supposed to feel passionately about in the meantime?

Free From Corporate America is about integrating the pursuit of dreams into your *current* life. Jon provides an actual game plan for re-inventing our careers and pursuing our passions *now*.

Acutely aware of the shortcomings of the scrimping and saving mentality, Jon provides a tactical plan for (1) building an economic foundation comprised of your own assets, and (2) integrating dream-chasing into your daily life. The subtitle of this book sums it up: it's all about success on your own terms.

To get us there, Jon introduces a number of fresh concepts:

• The redefinition of the word "asset" to *include* creative projects that could lead to income streams, and to *exclude* "false assets," such as homes that we are emotionally attached to and cars that offer more pleasure than value.

• "Stealing time" from your day-to-day life to ensure that you are building your own assets, and not just assets for your employer and debts for your creditors.

• Jon's "Law of Accumulation" that cuts both ways: *what you focus on is what you will become.* Spend a few hours each week on your own asset, and you've got something that could lead to financial self-sufficiency; spend a few hours each weekend pulling weeds, and you've become a de facto crabgrass aficionado.

• The "feedback loop" that will gauge marketplace demand for your asset, and ultimately mitigate risk.

• Getting in touch with your inner salesperson, whether or not you think you've got one or need one.

• "Personal branding" that puts your career ahead of your employer.

• "Barriers to entry" that are both obstacles to our dreams, and tools we can use to keep the competition at bay once we've entered a marketplace.

• Getting through "lag time," that stomach-churning, doubt-filled period between creating an asset and reaping its rewards.

• How to borrow "balance sheets" and other financial statements primarily used by businesses, and use them to take your own financial snapshot, assess the viability of assets you've created, and benchmark your progress over the years.

Jon learned these concepts the hard way. He wrote this book in response to all the bad ideas he accumulated over the years, many of which came from institutions that were supposedly charged with "educating" him. This, too, is something most of us can relate to: family "advice" that backfired, degrees that proved either irrelevant or inadequate, and employers that reaped the benefit of our work ethic but had a pink slip waiting for us.

When I first met Jon Reed eleven years ago, he was a rising star in the dotcom boom. He had built a lucrative niche in the world of SAP as a career counselor and market analyst. He was well on his way to an early retirement, when he would finally begin the process of fulfilling his dreams.

Like many of us who were riding high in the dotcom glory days, there were a few bumps in the road ahead for Jon – not the least of which would be the realization that postponing his creative life came at a high personal cost.

After the dotcom bust, Jon found himself self-employed, but facing similar challenges. This time, he was beholden to his clients instead of an employer. It was an improvement, but something was still missing. What he lacked was a methodology for achieving financial autonomy that integrated his passions into his daily life. Thus began Jon's journey into asset creation. For him, this included real estate, screenplays, and books, though he analyzed many other asset-development paths as well.

Those of you who follow Robert Kiyosaki and his *Rich Dad, Poor Dad* books will recall that Kiyosaki touches on similar themes, in terms of creating income-generating assets, and the need to shift from an employee's mentality to an owner's mentality. Kiyosaki addresses his readers from atop the mountain of professional and financial success.

Free From Corporate America comes from Jon's significantly different perspective, halfway up an altogether different kind of mountain. It's a climb that has exacted a cost, but has also afforded Jon the opportunity to analyze paths of ascension and identify the secrets of those who succeeded and those who failed in their attempts.

Jon wants us to learn from the mistakes he and others have made along the way: debt he acquired for the wrong reasons, feeling a sense of ownership of businesses he did not own, and back-burnering dreams for too long – dreams that contained important clues about a way forward that combined passion and marketability.

Jon took a different route for a reason: he wanted to chart out another kind of success, one that would allow us to define our own terms of engagement with the corporate world. Jon also wanted to see if the narrow definition of "assets" some books endorse could be expanded to include a more creative view of the kinds of assets you can cultivate and the kind of life you can construct around those assets.

After all, what is the use of becoming rich if you never feel any freer? And what is the point of accumulating wealth if doing so requires you to sign over your time, your values, and in some cases, your physical health in exchange for too many years in a cube?

The result is *Free From Corporate America.* Yes, integrating your dreams into your daily life is an ambitious task, but Jon has a plan. This does not necessarily mean quitting your day job and starting your own business.

The *Free From Corporate America* methodology is about developing a new mindset about your relationship to work, time, and your dreams, and wresting your fate from the Enrons (and future Enrons) of the world. And it's also about having a shoulder to lean on when the going gets tough.

This is one of those rare books on success where the author openly acknowledges his own defects and flaws. It comes as a bit of a shock, perhaps, that Jon does not minimize the adversity we will face and the odds we may (or may not) overcome. Jon doesn't romanticize our chances, but he gives us something better than happy talk: a strategy that is strong enough for life as it really is.

Free From Corporate America is an entertaining read, but not necessarily a comfortable one. It may even make you squirm. There will be a direct correlation between how much you are squirming and how much work you need to do.

You'll know you have already mastered a concept when you breeze through a chapter. You'll know you have room for improvement when you trip on a sentence, re-read, and feel a little shaken. Jon's goal is *not* to scare us into quitting our day jobs and selling our record collections, but he does want to inspire us into action.

This is a book for people like me who lie awake at night, dwelling on our financial future and dreams postponed, which is to say, 99% of the people I know. Whether you are an artist, an executive, or a stay-at-home mother, there is a *Free From Corporate America* concept you can integrate into your life today.

Rachel Meyers
Co-Author, Resumes From Hell
Westhampton, MA

Part I:

The End of the Corporate Contract

Why I Wrote This Book

Whom Is This Book for, and What Are Virtual Companies?

Are Small Businesses More Ethical Than Large Businesses?

"Most people who pat themselves on the back about values and business are full of it. Doing business in accordance with your values takes serious fortitude."

Why I Wrote This Book

The "corporate contract" has been broken. Today's workers are free agents who sink or swim on their own. I wrote *Free From Corporate America* for folks like me – people who want to succeed in business, but on their own terms. There is a lot to be said for the entrepreneurial life, but running your own business is a heck of a lot more difficult than the infomercial gurus would have us believe. And starting your own business is not the only way forward, either.

The last fifteen years have given me an opportunity to put business ideas to the ultimate test: do they pay the rent? I wanted to be successful without compromising my values or drinking the corporate Kool-Aid. When I graduated from college, I didn't know much, but I did know this: I didn't want anything to do with "pink slip culture." But of course that was easier said than done. It's tough to avoid getting snared in a 9 to 5 trap. Before you know it, you find yourself training your overseas replacement.

I'm going to use the phrase "pink slip culture" a lot, so I might as well define it. I see pink slip culture as the current state of white (and blue) collar work across the globe, where the vast majority of employees are in reality employees-at-will, who can (and will) be fired and replaced with cheaper alternatives whenever it is in their employers' best financial interests.

This "employed at will" doctrine is driven by the short term, results-oriented nature of the investment economy, where companies must manage their internal costs ruthlessly to ensure they are considered attractive to investors.

The best way to take a stand against pink slip culture is to adopt an entrepreneurial approach to your career. This does not necessarily mean starting your own business. It does mean developing skills and creating assets that may someday put you in a more marketable position. "Financial freedom" might be one end result, but most of us would settle for comfortable living on our own terms.

This book reveals tactics that have helped people I know change their circumstances, sometimes in dramatic fashion. I have found that many of these techniques are not commonly known or discussed. Some of them even go against conventional ideas about work, wealth and retirement. My goal? To come up with a practical guide to success on your own terms – one that is in step with today's "global economy."

Most of us want to attain a greater level of financial freedom, however we define it. But how do you get from professional struggle to a more powerful position? It's my hope that somewhere in this book lies a missing piece of the reader's puzzle. Whether it's the distinction between true and false assets or the difference between the employee's mindset and the owner's mindset; whether it's the concept of "lag" or the value of the "feedback loop," there should be some ideas in here that you haven't run into before. And they are not presented as random concepts, but as part of an overall methodology.

Countless misadventures went into this book's formation. As I wrote it, I recalled the ridiculous messes I've found myself in over the years. That's one good thing about adversity – it forces you to face what works and what doesn't. I can't say this book will work for everyone, but I will certify that it's built on proven tactics rather than get-rich-quick schemes.

Unlike other books on "success" that tell you what you want to hear, reassuring you that "if you dream it, you can do it," this book doesn't indulge those clichés. The fact is we may never get to where we want to go. It doesn't make sense to sugarcoat that. What we need is an anatomy of what we are up against. We need a plan of action we won't regret – even if the end result is not exactly what we intended.

The chapters on overcoming adversity and dealing with setbacks are based on the stinging reality that we might come up short despite our most passionate efforts. A truthful inventory of what we are good at (and whether we can ever get paid for it) is another necessary, if painful, part of this process.

I can't offer a smooth-talking guarantee, but this book will improve your chances of financial and professional success if you are willing to follow it. Of course, there is a catch: what I have outlined here is effective, but it's far from easy. As far as I can tell, there's no way around the sacrifices required for that truer kind of success that I, for one, have always craved.

In the past, there were easier choices that led to lives of comfort and contentment. The new instability of "9 to 5 America" has changed all that. The option to avoid risk in exchange for corporate stability has been taken off the table. What I am advocating used to be the riskier path with the higher upside. Now it is the safer path, and I'll explain why. But I'm not going to deny it: this way was never easy. Fortunately, creating your own livelihood has many unexpected rewards along the way.

Responding to the global economy is a complex business; I'm not trying to solve everyone's economic hardships, nor would I know how. But a lot of us are at the point where we don't know where to begin. Well, we can begin by taking matters into our own hands.

The best response is a creative one – one that draws on our strengths and relates directly to our so-called "core values." Most people who pat themselves on the back about values and business are full of it. Doing business in accordance with your values takes serious fortitude.

Your way will be different than mine, but we can all benefit from putting the most effective tactics in writing. And that's what *Free From Corporate America* is about.

"For the lifestyle entrepreneur, buying time is more important than accumulating cash. Beyond a certain comfort level, money has a diminishing return."

Whom Is This Book for, and What Are Virtual Companies?

I wrote this book for people who are done with pink slip culture and looking for more economic control. *Free From Corporate America* is based on years of knee-scraping escapes, so it's ideal for 9 to 5ers who have always wanted to step out but don't know where to begin. It's also handy for college grads who are just getting started in their careers but don't want to get snared in the live-to-work/work-to-live trap.

The "best practices" detailed in this book are also useful for freelancers of all stripes, especially those artistic types who are looking to give their business skills a little more bite.

Small business owners may also find a use for this book, though if you've already lived what I'm writing about, it will probably feel more like a confirmation of your own sensibilities than a bold new path.

But what if you are committed to a corporate career path and don't have time for side ventures? There are still some things you can do to brand yourself and boost your marketability *without leaving your current employer*. I'll get to those concepts later in the book. Starting your own business is *not* a requirement to put this book's principles into action.

This book would not have been possible without technical innovations that allow small companies to create niche services and compete in a wired world despite a disadvantage in resources or location.

"Virtual company" is a trendy term to describe small businesses, often home-based, that focus on a narrow competency and collaborate with partners online to deliver services to customers. Saying that you have a virtual company is a fancy way of saying that "location doesn't matter anymore."

That's not entirely true – many businesses are still dependent on relationships that require "face time." But these technical advances mean that we now have a better chance of structuring our businesses around our lifestyles than ever before. A friend of mine recently pulled off a virtual sleight-of-hand: she managed to take a nine day trip to Argentina without her employer knowing. All she had to do? Master the time zones and log into her instant messenger on schedule. When more employers open their minds to virtual workforces, such ruses will not be needed.

Of course, technology cuts both ways. If you've ever been BlackBerried by your boss while on vacation, you know exactly what I mean. But the Internet does make it possible to compete on a high level without a Manhattan street address.

Of course, there are different kinds of entrepreneurs with different agendas. For the purposes of this book, "Bill Gates Entrepreneurs" are folks who may be starting small but who have big corporate aspirations. They wouldn't mind running a big company someday and making that company their life's work.

I also put the "Build to Flip" types in this category. These are the folks who build companies to sell as soon as possible. Some build to flip folks want to cash out for good, but a surprising amount do it again and again, well past the point where they need the money. They live for the deal.

"Lifestyle Entrepreneurs," on the other hand, would be less inclined to sell their companies (what would they do next?), or if they do eventually sell, it will be the result of a slow build rather than an all-consuming push.

For the lifestyle entrepreneur, business is not the be-all; it is a means to an end. Financial success is important, but only to a point. Beyond that, shutting down the computer to train for a triathlon or take the brats to mini-golf is more important. For the lifestyle entrepreneur, buying time is more important than accumulating excess cash.

Beyond a certain comfort level, money has a diminishing return. If forced to choose, the lifestyle entrepreneur would probably trade a *Business Week* cover story for a rafting trip with college pals. And most would take $90,000 and a 30-hour work week over $150,000 and a 60-hour work week.

This book is geared toward the "lifestyle entrepreneurs," the people who want to put their business interests to work for them without losing themselves to their business. Since businesses tend to consume the participants, this is not an easy accomplishment.

"When you run your own show, you have one big advantage: you don't have to run decisions up some kind of idiotic flagpole."

Are Small Businesses More Ethical Than Large Businesses?

The inference is all over these pages: *small businesses are more ethical than large ones.*

Is this really true? Or is this just the arrogance of someone on the fringes of big business passing judgment on companies with more complex legal and financial requirements?

There may be a bit of that. When I talk with other small business owners, sometimes we do pat ourselves on the back too much because "we don't work for 'da man." But when you dig, you find that most small businesses depend upon larger entities for their survival. And most owners will concede: there's not much difference between a micro-managing boss and a micro-managing client. Either way, they're still running you.

I would take it further: at their worst, small business owners are some of the worst people on earth: dysfunctional "big fish/small pond" jerks who make the lives of their employees a living hell. Some of the worst experiences of my life came at the hands of small business owners drunk on their delusions.

By contrast, corporate managers tend to have more light shed on their indiscretions, either through performance reviews or through competition for higher-level positions. But when you run your own business, you have one big advantage: you don't have to run decisions up some kind of idiotic flagpole.

Example: A friend of mine was recently denied her bonus by a small-minded corporate HR department that lost sight of its purpose. It's a tedious and common story: bureaucrats and lawyers having inappropriate impact on business decisions. Turns out my company owed her a bonus too. Here the process was much simpler: I owed her a bonus so I paid her that bonus. I had the power to make the right choice, no rubber stamp required. My friend's supervisor, a ranking executive, wanted to do the same thing, but she was stuck in the corporate quagmire.

So do you have to share my values to take something from this book? No. But those who have strong convictions about how they want to do business and who want to have more control over their ventures will probably get the most out of this book.

I tend to have a pretty scathing view of large corporations, American or not. I am wary of the trick that publicly-held companies have played on themselves by being totally accountable, not to discredited mission statements, but to bottom-line-oriented shareholders. I am kind of old-fashioned: I happen to think you can only serve one god. No, you don't have to share my views to get something from this book. But let's face it, those in search of a quick buck can find an easier way than the one I'm about to lay out here.

Having said that, many of these tactics can be followed while working for large companies. And even when you're working for companies with ethical gray areas, there are departments and managers who have enough control to set their own tone. The ultimate test of values is not how large your employer is, but how your work stacks up against the person you wanted to be.

The fact is that big business has a lot to offer in terms of best practices that we can appropriate to achieve our own success. The financial section of this book is based largely on financial management practices I learned from working with larger companies. But I do find that nothing is more satisfying than ventures we have creative control over – and that's one thing big businesses cannot give us.

Following this book does not require anyone to change his or her values or to leave corporate America. But if you're looking for work that lines up better with your beliefs, you may find these tactics especially useful – no matter where you fall on the political spectrum.

When I hear people say that "those who don't do business ethically end up failing in the end," it makes me queasy. That doesn't jive with what I've seen. Sometimes bad deeds in business catch up with you, sometimes not. There's a bunch of Enron and WorldCom millionaires roaming around, coming soon to a putting green near you. And they are more than willing to share golf clubs with colleagues from more recent golden parachute embarrassments like Merrill Lynch and Lehman Brothers. Maybe what they did was legal, maybe not. But I can think of people who worked a lot harder and came out with a lot less. Business karma is either broken or much more complex than I can grasp.

You don't do business the right way because it's easier: you do it because you have a passion for treating people a certain way and will not bend on that point – even when it costs you financially. The good news? With the right approach, you can make good money without sleazing it up or biting your tongue. As for those who believe there's no way to succeed without selling out, I hope those grapes aren't too sour. They were the last time I ate them.

Part II:

Trapped by Pink Slip Culture

The Real Risk Is Working 9 to 5

You Don't Have to Live in the City to Be World Class

How Can I Possibly Advocate "Lifestyle Businesses" Given the Absurd Nature of My Own Existence?

Not All Debt Is Bad – It's How Hard You Can Swim That Counts

"In the global economy, paychecks are never too far from pink slips. A friend of mine works for a company where if you get up in the morning and can't log into the Extranet, you're either having technical problems or you've just been fired. You have to call tech support to find out."

The Real Risk Is Working 9 to 5

The working world is on its head. A corporate 9 to 5 gig is hardly secure; more and more Americans are taking the entrepreneurial plunge. But we can go further: the real risk now is working 9 to 5.

Workers can be generalized into two kinds of people: "9 to 5 types" prefer to work as an employee, performing a specific role for a finite period and clocking out. "Entrepreneurial types" play a higher stakes game. In exchange for the chance to cash out (and endure less micro-management), the entrepreneurs sign up for a different tradeoff: you don't get to leave your work at the office.

Thirty years ago, the two types had clear options: 9 to 5ers aligned themselves with a company "for life" and dug into a career; entrepreneurs started their own companies. Work has now turned on the 9 to 5 gang.

In the global economy, paychecks are never too far from pink slips. A friend of mine works for a company where if you get up in the morning and can't log into the Extranet, you're either having technical problems or you've just been fired. You have to call tech support to find out.

Companies pull a Catch-22 to justify their layoffs, claiming that workers have adopted a free agent mentality and can't be invested in for the long term. Since employees are (supposedly) no longer loyal, companies feel justified in reducing their obligations towards their employees accordingly. Meanwhile, most employees know the rules have changed but don't always know how to respond.

Of course, you can poke holes in these "two types of workers" generalizations. Food service is one obvious example of a profession that is outsourcing-proof. Contrary to the "Visit Starbucks.com" sign I saw recently outside of a Starbucks that had closed for the night, you can't do much about the coffee business online. There's a whole demographic of swell jobs in the "Subway Sandwich Artist" vein that are safe.

If recent experiences dealing with these individuals are any indication, baristas and sandwich artists don't take much comfort in their stability. Maybe if their wages were enough to support their families or vices they would.

And anyone who has had the joy of tracking down plumbers and electricians knows that tradespeople are also very comfortable with their work options and are feeling no urgency to get to your project site.

But in the white collar world, the threat of outsourcing is universal. Even doctors are running into the outsourcing of certain functions like medical tests and x-ray processing.

The entrepreneurial life is no longer the option for risk-takers; it is now the best choice for people with low risk tolerance. Those with high risk tolerance are advised to cling to their 9 to 5 jobs and say a prayer for big business.

Contrary to popular belief, you can also use an entrepreneurial approach while working for a large company. I know many consultants and managers who are thriving within large companies by shifting their mindset from "How can I help this company meet its insatiable need for increasing profit?" to "How can I make a contribution while enhancing my own skills, reputation, and visibility?" Later, we'll return to techniques you can use to inject a corporate career with entrepreneurial savvy.

The point is not to live in fear of pink slips; the point is to recognize that the seismic plates of employment have shifted. A creative and strategic response may not always save us, but it's probably more effective than denial.

Still, there are some valid questions: What about all the people who accept this argument but who are stuck on the treadmill? What if you have no time? What if it's all you can do to haul yourself out of bed, sinking feeling in your gut, and do it all over again?

Well, I can't do much for the dread, except to say that I've felt it and probably we all have. But what I can do is publish this book. And most of the book will be about taking those first key steps off the corporate hamster wheel, when time and resources are scarce.

"It's a mistake to get too hung up on location: you can make a mess of your life anywhere. It's the sum of your strategy and performance that counts."

You Don't Have to Live in the City to Be World Class

I know some big city lovers who think that because they live amongst celebrities, they have a better chance of success.

It may be reassuring to wait in line next to Jennifer Aniston, but from the vantage point of this book, big city living might even be a disadvantage – until you reach a point when you are ready to capitalize on a market you have defined.

Technology changed the equation. Not long ago, Rachel Meyers and I did a book interview shoot at a local news studio. Via a fiber line, they shot a segment on our book *Resumes From Hell,* which aired on CNN. Media coverage now has more to do with relentless marketing (and a good story) than convenience of location.

The advantage of a city like New York or Los Angeles is the "relationship factor": connections lead to good breaks. But here's the catch: *you can only leverage those connections after you have a track record.* First you need a finished work product, *then* you can sell it. If your product is good enough and you're not afraid to work the room, you can make connections when you need them. It's a lot more satisfying to hand David Sedaris a copy of your book than to give him a sweaty "I'm a big fan" handshake.

The problem with the city is its financial grip. Maintaining a low cost of living is critical to the early-to-mid stages of freeing yourself from corporate America. If you can't keep expenses low, it's hard to fund those early stage ventures. When it takes 15 minutes to grab a carton of milk, you have a productivity obstacle. My office is a two-minute walk from my house, and so it goes for most aspects of small town life.

When I get to the point where more projects are finished and ready for palm pressing, I'll hit the city. No question there are advantages to urban living, but it's a mistake to get too hung up on location: you can make a mess of your life anywhere. It's the sum of your strategy and performance that counts. No matter where you live – and you can put the principles of this book into practice in any "free" market – you want to be a world-class expert in your chosen skill area.

The market is a tough place with little tolerance for bad ideas and shallow pockets. That's why, when you think of freeing yourself from corporate America, you're talking about finding (or creating) a niche that large companies can't afford to serve or can't move fast enough to claim.

In *Good to Great*, author Jim Collins details his findings: the most successful companies must be the best in the world at something close to their core business. His results are based on a study of publicly-held companies, but the same logic applies to small, virtual companies.

To compete against the big players, you need to have a best-in-the-world niche. If you're not currently the best, you either need to drop that focus or a make a commitment to excellence until you get there. You should be able to explain, in a sound bite, why larger companies are not in position to mimic your business model and send you back to the lab or the unemployment line.

Too many of us head to the unemployment line. Go back to the lab instead. Business re-invention is not easy, but we often come up with our best ideas after taking a pounding from the market.

Location matters, but strategy matters more. If we truly become "world class" in a particular area, we can ride that expertise for a long time. I've milked an expertise in SAP software trends for a decade now. Without that niche, I'd be just another freelance writer pitching columns on high-tech razors while dodging my landlord.

"To enter the economic world without an economic strategy makes no sense. To see yourself as an employee in a world that caters to business owners is an even more terrible mistake. I made both of them."

How Can I Advocate "Lifestyle Businesses" Given the Absurd Nature of My Own Existence?

I can hear the people who know me stifling a laugh. How can I possibly advocate "lifestyle businesses" given the absurd nature of my own existence?

Fair enough: I wouldn't wish my lifestyle on anyone. But I have no doubt that these principles can be successfully adopted by folks with a more balanced approach. One of my role models is an Internet book publisher who makes a very good living in his underwear. He optimizes his Web site for Google when he gets bored.

It bothers me when people turn away from these ideas because of how hard I work. The only reason I work like I do is because I made some fateful decisions long ago that turned into a pretty big hole. Don't step into the hole, and you won't have to work like I do.

So where did I veer off? To sum up this cautionary tale, I was not raised to be an entrepreneur. And in the global economy, if you don't understand the entrepreneurial approach to life, you probably won't succeed.

Even if you do, your success will be precarious, as it will be based on the blessing of fickle institutions rather than on ownership of your own creations. These are strong statements, but I'll back them up before this book is done.

It's possible to be educated and have no clue: I graduated from college with absolutely no idea how to finance my creative ventures.

The job I was most qualified for? Grocery bagger. My degree had an astonishing impotence, but I didn't wake up. I idealized the fact that I had no strategy and no financial competence. I would simply "do what I loved" and "the money would take care of itself."

To enter the economic world without an economic strategy makes no sense. To see yourself as an employee in a world that caters to business owners is an even more terrible mistake. I made both of them. Even when you're somebody's employee, you must never lose your "owner's consciousness." There has to be a side project out there with your name on it; you need an asset to call your own. Simple? It took me a decade to get that, and that's ten years *after* I graduated from college. I know some professors who should be ashamed of themselves. On second thought, does the problem start even higher?

The "do what you love" doggerel of liberal arts fantasyland haunted me well into my twenties. When the bill for those illusions came due, it was mighty steep.

I can't romanticize my own bad decisions either. I call those self-limiting acts "piling on"; it's the worst form of betrayal you can feel. One thing worse than my own predicament was watching my friends twist in the economic wind. If I had hunkered down in academia I might have found a comfort zone, but then again, comfort zones are breeding grounds for mediocrity. Academia can be a great career, but for me, it would have been a cop-out.

Now, at 39, I'm a long way towards digging out. The excavation is still a 24/7 project. The reason I push so hard? I'm determined to live a life beyond the stereotype of the meek, "I'll settle for this," white-collar existence that some seem to find acceptable but I see as total capitulation. I know it (and it's not fun to type this) because I've lived it.

Disclaimer: one of the biggest misconceptions of all is that you succeed in life by outworking people. The upcoming phrase whiffs of cheese, but the corporate trainers are right: "working smarter" is more important, and we'll return to that theme.

For now, let's steal one from Charles Barkley: "I am not a role model." You can appropriate these philosophies without becoming Jon Reed. Think of me as an overweight gym teacher; you can make these moves a lot more athletically than I did.

"At certain points in your business career, you will run into an opportunity that lies beyond your means. If you borrow in order to seize that chance, I consider that to be strategic debt, which is vastly different than flat screen TV debt."

Not All Debt Is Bad – It's How Hard You Can Swim That Counts

Financial mismanagement is a major problem in business. Talented people toil in obscurity. More often than not, these struggles can be traced back to bad ideas about how to approach the money side of a venture.

The way people manage a business is closely related to how they manage their own finances. Most of us could have used more school time on finance and less time memorizing our state's governors – not to pick on my own teachers or anything... Mr. Alexander!

There are two mentalities when it comes to personal finances. "Cash is king" folks don't worry about consumer debt; they rely on it to finance must-have purchases like no money down flat screens. Their thinking: as long as you can make the payments, why not live a little? Grain of truth: cash truly is king in business. A strong cash flow *does* overcome many obstacles.

There is a problem with the cash is king mentality, though: debt-financed creature comforts bloat the monthly budget. Now you're locked into high-income jobs just to keep the ship afloat. That's a recipe for getting latched onto corporate America, *not* for breaking free.

Then there's the "debt is bad/live within your means" crowd. These folks use debit cards to buy a bottle of water or a pack of gum; the rest of us wait in line behind them. But you have to admire the fiscal discipline. They know what leaves their wallet and where it goes. The problem with this approach? Not all debt is bad. The live within your means lifestyle is practical, but it tends to be fear-based, the equivalent of a squirrel forever gathering nuts.

Here's the problem: at certain points in your business career, you will run into an opportunity that lies beyond your means. If you borrow in order to seize that chance, I consider that to be "strategic debt," which is vastly different than "flat screen TV debt." Both might end up on credit cards, but not all credit card debt is created equal.

Merge these two approaches. The cash-flow-is-king mentality is valid but requires a better appreciation of the difference between good and bad debt, as well as the fiscal discipline of living within your means. Meanwhile, the avoid-debt-at-all-costs approach holds you back when big deals go down. It's too bad most people fall firmly into one camp or the other, because the two extremes make a good mix.

One of my earliest business mentors was Tom Turley. Tom ran a printing press called Turley Publications. He took a liking to me despite my obvious ignorance. During my last meeting with him, he made a point of saying: "Remember, Jon, it's not how deep the water is, it's how hard you can swim." I took that to mean two things: you can handle some debt, and don't be afraid of the deep end of the pool.

Of course, it's not as simple as good debt versus bad debt. It's a continuum with disposable purchases on one side (such as vacations) and strategic purchases on the other (such as equipment to serve a client who just signed a service contract with you).

I financed my first computer on credit cards, back when computers were not as cheap as snowboards. It was *not* the best kind of business debt because I didn't have any paying customers. I didn't even know what a paying customer looked like. A couple of "live within your means" friends criticized me for that risk (though I noticed they had no crisis of conscience using my new equipment). I'm not going to lie: it was a struggle to pay that debt down.

Taking that risk was part of my business education. I wasn't a strong swimmer at first, but by God, I was in the water. Brazen risk is irresponsible, but strategic risk is the defining factor.

Part III:

Developing Assets

So Where Do You Begin? On Risk Tolerance and Asset Creation

First Step: Claiming a Space for Your Project

Time Is the Ultimate Commodity

Stealing Time Versus Paying the Rent

Understanding the Law of Accumulation

What If You Don't Want to Start Your Own Business?

"There was a time when Harry Potter was just a manuscript also. But assets with no established value are speculative assets. Speculative assets are riskier, and we can't delude ourselves on this point."

So Where Do You Begin?
On Risk Tolerance and Asset Creation

So what if you accept my argument? What if you concede that the working world has flipped and the real risk is working 9 to 5? Does that mean you quit your job and start your own business tomorrow? Not necessarily.

True, plenty of entrepreneurs were pushed into starting their own companies through pink slips – myself included – but that can be an icy plunge. It's not easy to find the time to start a company when you're working full time, but your current salary gives you protection (and early stage financing) during the most vulnerable periods in the startup process.

A big mistake is defining your startup options too narrowly. The business gurus mess this up on their infomercials also. Breaking free from corporate America is about creating assets of your own. But there are all kinds of assets. An asset can be a piece of real estate or a customer database, but it can also be a screenplay or an unpublished manuscript.

Let's not be dreamy: not all "assets" are created equal. An unpublished piece of writing or a painting in your basement has questionable market value. In the end, your assets must achieve financial value in order to be deserving of that word. You must take your work to market.

We can think of assets on a continuum, with proven assets such as residential real estate on one extreme, and a book of unpublished poems on the other. Accountants might even call some of these assets "intangible," but I don't agree. It's hard to say what's intangible these days. Goodwill and business reputation, for example, used to be considered intangible assets, downgraded accordingly when businesses were assessed by prospective buyers.

But in the branding age, it's the hard-to-quantify brand name of a business that dictates much of its purchase price during an acquisition. (Many point to the acquisition of Kraft by Philip Morris in 1988 for $12.9 billion – six times Kraft's net asset value – as the dawn of a new age in the perceived value of intangible assets such as brand names.) In the end, an asset is worth what someone is willing to pay for it.

It's fair game to devote your energy to the creation of assets which have an uncertain market value. There was a time when Harry Potter was just a manuscript also. But assets with no established value are "speculative assets." Speculative assets are riskier, and we can't delude ourselves on this point. But here's the good news: there are ways to moderate that risk.

Just how speculative an asset is depends on a host of factors, including your marketing skills, budget and creative talent. This book is a speculative asset; I have no idea how it will be received. Since I make money on my other books, I hope to make money on this book also. But there is always a risk when you devote time to creating something without a proven market.

In theory, I could have reduced my risk if I had stopped writing after a few chapters and secured a book deal, perhaps through an agent. If I had held off on sinking more time into this project until I had financing from a publisher, then I could have reduced the risk by receiving a cash advance for the time invested.

Another way to reduce the risk on a speculative asset is to invoke the feedback loop and use the Internet to gauge the level of demand for your product or service. This is a type of soft launch, an affordable way to map out a possible market. We'll get into this in more detail in the "Internet Changes Everything" chapter.

When you find a third party willing to mitigate your risk, they will ask for a healthy piece in return. That's why the upside for this book is significantly higher if I either (a) sell it through my company (at a much higher net margin than I could get from a larger publisher), or (b) *wait and sell it to a larger publisher when I have already established a market demand and can negotiate more favorable terms.*

Because I have assumed the risk of proving this book has a market, I will be in a much better negotiating position down the line. (Though in this case, the main reason I am publishing it myself is because I don't see how I can write about freedom from corporate America without total editorial control.)

Risk tolerance comes down to the individual. Because I am relatively stable in my financial situation, I am able to tolerate a higher degree of risk and finance my own book ventures. Therefore, with my speculative creative assets, I can afford to hold out for a higher level of return.

Taking my own advice, why wouldn't I just buy real estate with my extra money instead of financing my creative projects? Why sink money into a speculative asset when you can purchase a conventional one? Valid point: it *would* make more sense for me to get involved in real estate. Real estate is one of the most lucrative investments in proportion to risk, since the paper asset is secured by a property with a (usually) stable value.

I don't get involved with real estate for one reason: my passion lies elsewhere. Beware of starting something on the side that you are not truly passionate about. I do enjoy real estate investment and have done a fair amount of it, but I decided to pursue a dream in publishing. That's the trickiest part of this whole *Free From Corporate America* thing: *you have to strike a balance between the skills most in demand and the skills you most want to master.*

And that brings us back to the "Do what you love and the money will follow" approach. Is that what I am endorsing here? In a word, no. "Do what you love" only works if you are fortunate enough to have passions that line up with the marketplace. Let's take two examples: I know a lawyer who wanted to prosecute rapists and sex offenders even while she was in college. This motivation led her into a legal career working with non-profits and she has no regrets. The money isn't outstanding, but it's good enough. Her occupational passion is decently aligned with the marketplace.

But what if you hate your job, as many do, and you live to garden? Fresh vegetables might improve your quality of life, but you can garden for decades without making money, unless you feel like running a vegetable stand. To turn a life in gardening into a profitable business, you'd have to refine your approach. You could write a book on gardening, or you could get into some type of organic food business, or even landscape design or floral arranging.

There are some interests you just can't squeeze a dollar from – try being a musician. Yes, you can tweak the model by playing in a cover band or opening a recording studio or publishing a music newsletter (all true life examples I've seen), but the music biz is still a tough nut to crack, dominated by top-down interests.

If there was a huge market for thirtysomething wannabe rock musicians, that's probably what I'd be pursuing. But the joy I get from music is not from proximity to the industry but from playing original material. And there are musicians a lot better than me struggling to make ends meet. Fact: I would need vast resources to take the edge off near-impossible odds, so for me, music rightly falls into the hobby category.

There's a place in life for interests outside the marketplace. But if you're up for it, most passions can be transformed into marketable pursuits if you are willing to play different roles than you might have originally envisioned (for example, selling songs to other artists as opposed to trying to make it in your own band). It's all a matter of what falls within your business goals and, of course, if it crosses your own line in the sand about what you're willing to sell and what you're not. Some musicians have no problem playing Bar Mitzvahs; others would see that as a personal apocalypse.

So on our continuum of speculative-to-marketable assets, we should develop the most marketable assets that jive with our interests. Passion does matter: I know a lot of folks who run businesses they can't stand. Sometimes I feel pretty sorry for them. On bad days, I'm one of them. But it's equally foolish to work on self-indulgent projects in the naïve hope that the market will someday smile on you because you love your work and therefore deserve to be successful.

Unless you have genius-level talent, you can't get away with Albert Einstein's "lost in the lab" tunnel vision. You need to master more than asset creation; you also need to know how to bring that asset to market and how similar assets are valuated. You have to know your industry and/or your neighborhood and/or your competition.

I have a friend in New York who recently shot an animated short for submission to a comedy network. This project might seem like a long shot, except for the fact that he knows his industry inside and out. He has inside relationships, he has an agent, and he has studied the craft of script-writing and knows how to write for TV shows.

An animated short is certainly a speculative asset, but my buddy has lessened that risk through mastery of his craft and knowledge of his industry. He is also a stand-up comic, which has set up a valuable feedback loop that lets him know right away just how good his material is. We all need some kind of feedback loop; talent alone won't cut it. And we need to apply that talent through the best practices in our line of work.

Sometimes that feedback loop brings tough news: we may have a passion for things we don't excel at. I love to paint but have never been much good at it. I paint well only through over-the-top effort and lots of crummy sketches in the trash. Writing, on the other hand, comes more easily. But that's just a starting point: I still have to work at my craft, not to mention the editing process and how I fit into the publishing industry as a whole.

I know, for example, that it's a lot easier to self-publish a successful non-fiction book than a novel. I'd like to publish a novel someday too, but I've decided to put that off since the market obstacles are bigger. And when I do go after fiction, I'll probably pursue screenplays, as the market for screenplays is more clearly defined than the market for novels. I've learned this through my own homework.

Your interests are likely different, so your homework will be different. But as you consider the priorities I have set, it should give you a reference point as you find a balance between market trends and your own work preferences. And you do have to strike a balance.

I'm sure I could have chosen a more marketable non-fiction book than this one, perhaps a guide to abdominal exercise equipment. But I believe in this project. So I chose non-fiction as a genre, but I didn't choose the most marketable non-fiction topic of all time. On the other hand, I did set aside a more obscure, half-finished philosophy project for this business-oriented book, which I see as having a broader appeal. I found a way to write a book I could market that I also have a serious stake in.

In the end, pursuing the work you are most engaged with is the best idea, even if the odds are steeper. Why? Because in the world of virtual companies, we succeed when we are the best in the world at what we do. And you can't become great at something without continuously refining your skills. You do this by putting your most appealing business ideas in play and learning from the hard knocks. Even if you're met with silence, that's a heck of a message in its own way.

You may have to float a few projects before you see a pushback from the market. Once you see that first trickle of demand, you'll know you're headed in a good direction. With luck and effort, that trickle may become a revenue stream supported by an asset you own and control. You may or may not need a full time job at that point, but if you do, you will surely go to work better insulated against the whims of companies that hire and fire at will.

"The best part is not about business; it's about blowing the roof off of the limitations you have set on yourself. It's humbling to look back on a space you created when your plans felt more like reckless hopes."

First Step: Claiming a Space for Your Project

So you have an idea for an asset you'd like to create. It might be a business; it might be a manuscript; it might be a documentary film. You've decided this project is the best balance between your talents, finances, and eventual target market. Two likely (and not so small) problems: you don't know where to begin or how you're going to find the time to pull it off. We'll cover the time angle in the upcoming pages – this chapter focuses on where to start.

The first step may sound idiotically simple: create a space for your project. Projects don't gain momentum until they have a dedicated space. Ideally, this space will have a physical dimension, such as turning part of your apartment into a home office. But the space can be as simple as a new filing system, or even some new folders on your hard drive.

Some people start by writing business plans. I think that's usually a mistake (more on this in a later chapter). There is something irrational but magical that happens when you build your own space. Sometimes this first space can be in "cyberspace." Sometimes it can even be a slam dunk business name. I have an upcoming book planned with Rachel Meyers that I wasn't excited about until she told me the book title she had in mind. The title changed everything. It turned the project from mundane to exciting. A brilliant business name can do the same thing. When you take it a step further and register that business as a DBA, it can really focus your motivations.

Quick launches get you going. Instead of spending months on a professionally-designed Web site, it's often better to throw up something basic and start developing your content and marketing approach. Even if no one else can see it yet, it feels good to log on and check out the first incarnation of your new venture. I don't want to get too mystical, but when you create a space in the real world somewhere, you also create room in your imagination to begin seeding your project and envisioning the next steps.

I might not be in business today if someone hadn't forced this concept on me. The year was 1993; I decided to leave the publication I helped launch after college and go out on my own. I had some half-baked idea about bookkeeping and design services that I would tie into a "consulting business." Money was a problem. I decided to set up a temporary office on the dining room table of my apartment.

My roommate balked. He wanted to use the dining room table for dinners with his girl (he did end up marrying her, so I guess those dinners were kind of important). My roommate did me a heck of a favor, because the stand-off compelled me to rethink my options. I soon stumbled onto a tiny office above my old employer.

I wouldn't have considered an office if my roommate had let me get away with the dining room table, but as soon as I stepped into that dank little space, there was no looking back. It was outside my budget, so I had to finance part of the rent on credit cards. Putting rent on credit cards is not the best strategic risk, but investing in that space made me look at myself differently. From then on, I spent more time in that office than at home. Some of my happiest memories are curled up in a sleeping bag on that floor, grabbing a nap before another push.

The risk I took was on the speculative side, but there was a huge payoff: I was energized by that space. If I had started my business on the dining room table, I would not have put in the same hours. Renting that office gave me a "do or die" mentality. Eventually, my skills caught up with my ambition and I was able to get things right financially.

When I think back on my career so far, many of the biggest milestones had to do with creating a new space or a new image that upped the ante in some way. My first laptop, my first suit. The best part is not about business; it's about blowing the roof off of the limitations you have set on yourself. It's humbling to look back on a space you created when your plans felt more like reckless hopes.

After *Resumes From Hell* came out, I bought a new desktop file to organize our fledgling marketing efforts. Recently, we got national coverage on CNN and in the *New York Daily News*. Those were nice moments, but we started with some blank letterhead, back when nobody gave a thought to the project besides Rachel and myself. The real gratification is knowing you had the faith to see your project through. We are still working to get *Resumes From Hell* where we want it to be, but the victories can't be taken away either.

Marking out your territory is just the first step. I've done it many times and had it come to nothing. There is still the matter of follow-through. But you have to start somewhere. I'll concede that this is the most mystical aspect of this book. All I can say is try it and see for yourself what happens. Maybe you're invoking the gods of business; maybe you're just sending a message that you're finally ready to take your ventures seriously. To the skeptics I would say: if it works, why question it?

"The wealthiest people in the world are the ones who have control over how (and where) they spend their time. If you're making money but working your tail off year in/year out, then the system still owns you."

Time Is the Ultimate Commodity

Time is now the ultimate commodity. The wealthiest people in the world are the ones who have control over how (and where) they spend their time. If you're making money but working your tail off year in/year out, then the system still owns you. Of course, there are those who hate their jobs but are intentionally saving more than they spend. That's probably how most folks define their retirement planning.

I tip my hat to anyone who can bank more than they can squander, but if it takes 80 hours a week to do it, it's a heck of a gamble. Whenever you sacrifice too much for the demands of workaday living, money in the bank is little consolation. Time – not in the future but in the present – is the true badge of success.

When your time is spent on the people and projects that are most important to you, and when you work only because you find that work compelling, then you have achieved a rare and important freedom. This is an impressive accomplishment because it involves more than revenues – it involves self-mastery on almost every level, including emotional self-mastery, victory over expensive vices, and financial competence. Protecting your time and spending it wisely requires a much broader commitment than does a narrow focus on financial benchmarks.

In the last chapter, we talked about the importance of creating space for new projects. Unfortunately, that's the easy part. The next step involves actual implementation of the new idea, and that's where we falter. Wishing we had more time is easier than finding a way. There's no simple step forward, but mastering several concepts related to time will make a huge difference.

For the rest of our lives, we can count on a scarcity of time. At no point is this scarcity more dangerous than when we are stuck in a rut we are desperate to get out of. Wondering how we will find the time to plot a new course can make us more desperate. How are we ever going to pull it off?

"I'm a pessimist," one friend told me, before he downed another drink. As someone who has lost a lot of years to "comfortably numb," I know how he feels. But a belief in your own limitations is a self-fulfilling prophecy. If you don't believe you can alter the outcome, then why bother? That's why a good strategy is so important. Knowing you have the right plan can be the difference between one drink before bed and an all-night bender. When morale is higher, we make better decisions about time.

There are four key concepts about time to master. The first, time management, is obvious, and I won't spend much time on it here. The second, time stealing, and the third, the law of accumulation, are potent ideas I will address in the next chapters. The fourth one, time/money crossover, is a later stage concept I'll touch on down the road.

For now, let's do a breezy, no-PowerPoint review of time management. As I see it, "time management" refers to proven tactics that people can master to make the most out of the time they have. The key here is eliminating as many inefficiencies as we can in order to have the most time to spend at our discretion. I've spent years perfecting my daily/weekly organizational systems. The best systems are ones you devise to fit your own circumstance. Some people are visual list-makers like me, others prefer electronic tools and reminder prompts about upcoming tasks.

Generally speaking, I find that skillful prioritizing is the key to getting stuff done – along with a comfort-level that most projects will remain unfinished from week to week. We're all too busy to get much done on any given day; there is an art to knowing when to push ahead and when to regroup. I used to attack projects each week with the goal of completing them all.

I've finally gotten it through my thick skull: there's never enough time to get everything done. Making the right choices from day to day (and letting the unfinished stay unfinished) is the key. When I'm at my best, I'm "flowing" from project to project without staying up all night trying to get closure when there is none to be had.

It's not easy to leave things open-ended, especially when you're obsessed with closure like I am, but let's face it: you can't balance projects on the side without a bit of Zen-like patience that accepts "it takes the time it takes." That mentality doesn't come easy for me, but I've found a way to be a little more Zen and let the projects move at their own pace.

Time is too important a resource not to bring all your logistics to bear upon it. For most of us, there *are* inefficiencies that can be rooted out. To use a couple examples from my own life: for several years, commuting time took vital hours from my day. When I had the chance to get my own office, I made sure it was close to my house so I could reclaim that time.

More recently, I figured out some techniques for drip-drying my hair, even in the winter, with a minimum of blow drying. This may sound dorky – OK, it is pretty dorky – but when my hair was at my longest, that was twenty minutes a day I used to spend messing with wet tangles Any time you can save in the cash-strapped present, without impacting your quality of life, is gold. You can then invest that time towards the development of assets that can change your life.

Planning is another component. On Saturdays, I geek out over my calendar for the upcoming week. I almost always identify some overlapping commitments – things that need to be shuffled around or combined into one trip across town. The main purpose of this look ahead is to see if I can earmark time for creative projects. If I have too many pending appointments, I push some back to ensure I have time to write.

If you think this kind of fine-tuning sounds tedious, I'd say you're absolutely right. But it's better than running out of time. And as we'll see, sometimes the difference between parachuting out of your current career versus having to jump without one is just a matter of a few hours a week.

Of course, before you fight for your time, you have to believe in yourself and what you're fighting for. Usually, our biggest challenge is not a lack of dreams. Most of us have no problem dreaming big, but over time, our dreams poison us; we have no idea how to get there. The other shoreline looks as far as it ever did. And from that state of despair or resignation, we squander our time. Or perhaps we are still young and assume that we can have our fun for now, and later close the gap whenever we feel like it. But that's not how it works.

Without the right tactics, time has no obvious value to us. At that point, we waste time indiscriminately to avoid staring at the wall, or perhaps a mirror. Worse yet, we might head off in the wrong direction to avoid the discomfort of standing still. Time is a resource only when we know how to use it. That's why I believe that the right tactics are more important to our morale (and ultimate success) than any other factor. And the biggest tactic of all is taking control of our time.

We spend all kinds of time fussing over our cars, our lawns, our kids. We owe it to ourselves to do the same over our own time, developing systems to spend it better – understanding, of course, that drooling on the couch is an important part of each week also. It's not about becoming automated work machines, but it is about making conscious choices in the context of an overall strategy we believe in.

In the next chapters, we'll take a closer look at some advanced concepts pertaining to time that can make a huge difference in how to get these vital side ventures up and running in the midst of the daily grind.

"I used to have these rosy ideas that I would get a week or two at the end of the year and 'crank out a screenplay.' Or I would save enough money to take a year off and write my first book. It's pretty talk, but it's the talk of fools."

Stealing Time Versus Paying the Rent

Time works best when we are "in the flow." Being in the flow, as I define it, simply refers to times in your life when you are able to focus on projects that serve your own best interest. Whether it's a successful law career or cranking out a couple of kids, time is at its best when each day furthers our skills and interests.

Time is at its deadliest when our days are filled with the wrong work. These are the dreaded "treadmill" periods. Before we know it, months have turned into years, and we are further and further from who we wanted to be.

Even at the worst points, it's possible to master time, but it takes an enormous amount of faith and patience. You literally have to defy what you see around you, ignoring the evidence that you've lost the battle. Indeed, you may have lost the battle. Conceding that may hurt like hell. Concede, but don't capitulate. Sometimes it's hard to assess where we stand; this is the maddening "one step forward, two steps back" way of life.

Time is complicated: you have to judge your relationship to time based on a number of factors, including how much your time is worth, how much you love your work, and how much your work takes out of you. I don't exactly score the best grades in these areas myself. It's good to have stable clients and my own company, but I'm still at the point where the value of my time is not enough to save me from a lot of heavy hours in front of the computer. I like the work to a point, but I feel chained to it more often than not.

How to increase the value of your time and make your business work for you is a worthy discussion. But for this chapter, let's assume that whatever we're doing to pay the bills now is not our ideal profession, but a transitional occupation of some kind. So, how do we complete that transition? Take me for example: I hope to eventually spend all my time writing and/or marketing my own books. So how do I get there when my current workload crushes me all too often?

The answer lies in the tactic I call "stealing time." To lay the groundwork for a better life, we need to find the time *within our current lives* to develop the assets that will someday support us. We need to figure out, week in and week out, how we can steal some time to apply to forward-thinking projects. The more time we are able to spend on forward projects, the sooner we will get there – but there is always a significant waiting period. If you're as time-strapped as I am, I have some good news: the key is not how much time you can claim each week, but how consistently you claim it.

We spend most of our time on activities I call "paying the rent." Some of this work truly is tied to our ability to pay the rent or mortgage, but I use this phrase more broadly. I use "pay the rent" to encompass all the things we must do each week to keep our lives afloat. This includes time we spend on exercise, family, grooming, and commuting as well as work. It even includes some time on the couch.

Rest is part of the weekly cycle, and we ignore that at our own peril. Some entrepreneurs steal time by cheating their families or their bodies out of maintenance time. It's an approach that has come back to haunt a lot of folks. It might work for a short period, but this book is about the long haul, and for the long haul, paying the rent is part of the deal, and the "rent" includes what others expect from us each day.

Now, there are some things we might initially classify as paying the rent that we are better off paying someone else to do: lawn care comes to mind. When it comes to stealing time, we're on the lookout for any time we can claim that is not already earmarked for something important. Any time leftover once we've paid the rent and fulfilled our obligations is fair game.

Reasonable goals are the best. With this book, I aimed for one chapter a week, then changed it to one every two weeks. I missed some targets, mostly due to illness or traveling. But when I was in town and on my game, I was able to steal the time for a chapter every two to three weeks. That's all it comes down to. I like to call it stealing time because it sounds a lot sexier than what it really is. But I think it's a fair term to use, because even if the process is dull sometimes, the end result sure is magical.

When you find time for next-phase projects, you feel something shift. My morale goes up for days when I find time to work on crucial projects. Developing future assets sends a strong message that I'm not giving up despite the odds. Finding a way to do that while maintaining my other commitments makes me feel like I just might be OK after all. We need to feel like the systems we have in place are functional, not dysfunctional.

I used to have these rosy ideas that I would get a week or two at the end of the year and crank out a screenplay. Or I would save enough money to take a year off and write my first book. Sound familiar? It's pretty talk, but it's the talk of fools. We succeed when we find a way to insert forward-thinking time into our daily (or weekly) routines.

As for me, I don't always know when my opportunity to write is going to hit. I don't really have a set schedule. What I have is a series of daily and weekly priorities. Each week, after I get on top of my client projects, I start looking for an hour or two when I can take my laptop on the town.

I also try to protect Sundays as a writing day, though sometimes real life interferes. My time-on-the-fly approach might not work for everyone, but this is the third book I have completed in the midst of ridiculous work commitments, so I must be doing something right.

Others have different approaches. Sometimes more structure is the way to go. I know a painter who sets his alarm one hour before his kids get up. What I can say for sure is that consistency is the key. Stealing time is a lot like weight loss – the dramatic diets that yield quick results often fall apart, whereas the lifestyle changes that support better nutrition for the long haul reap bigger dividends.

There are all kinds of ways to steal time. I've done some good work on this book while sitting next to Bob Barker/Drew Carey fans at the car dealership. I juxtapose stealing time with paying the rent because it's easy to beat ourselves up over all the things we don't get done each week. But there are certain commitments we have to look after first, and that includes helping friends in need and lugging cats to the vet. We have to go easy on ourselves when it comes to living a full life.

If we don't work our bigger plans into the flow of our lives, we'll be stuck with pipe dreams. The key is letting go of the "Somedays": "Someday I'll have time to do this or that; Someday I'll have the right place/city/job." Most people who aren't fixing their lives now will never get around to it.

It's hard to accept that we're no better than our present moment, but that's also where the opportunity lies. It's just that our big chance is grittier than we expected (or were told it would be), so it's understandable we don't recognize it even though it's right in front of us.

It turns out that being busy is just one more excuse not to get started. Legend has it that Pulitzer Prize winner Toni Morrison wrote her first book, *The Bluest Eye*, with her kids swarming around her ankles. Turns out she actually wrote most of it while her two sons were asleep, but the point stands: if Toni had decided that between her day job and her kids she was too busy to write a book, all of her friends would have soothingly supported that rationalization. But she didn't let herself off that hook.

For years, I kept waiting for the perfect time to write. It never came. If anything, life got more hectic and more difficult. Time got scarcer. But now I steal time to write even in the worst of times, even when there is good reason not to. I write when I'm sick; I write when I'm lonely; I write when I'm utterly discouraged. And the work adds up.

It's amazing how many people refuse to get started on big plans because they think they have no time. What they really have is no belief in how a few hours a week, week in and week out, can eventually change everything. No question: it takes a lot of fortitude to gut your way through the early periods of such projects. But once you get in a groove, you'll see that stealing time is worth it just for the psychological benefits.

When you take your time seriously, good things start to happen. I find that my relationships improve also. It's hard to be a force for good in the world when you have nothing to live for and nothing to defend. When you decide your time is worth protecting, it sets off a chain reaction where you no longer have room in your life for people who don't have your best interests at heart.

Perhaps the reason people are so closed to this kind of approach is that we hunger for a get-rich-quick scheme, a scratch ticket for human achievement. I just got an email from a Web site visitor: "Show me how to get a big return with no money down." If only.

It really is easier to throw drinks at problems rather than soldier towards some elusive goal. Those like me with little faith will be tested the most. I know I am still daunted by the odds sometimes. But it can be done, and at certain points, your life depends on it – certainly your hopes of a better life do.

"The phrase 'jack of all trades, master of none' used to be an insult. In the global economy, it's a death sentence."

Understanding the Law of Accumulation

The Law of Accumulation may be the most terrifying concept in this book. Unlike the other ideas I have advocated, this law is in effect whether we choose to apply it or not.

The Law of Accumulation is a fancy way of saying that *what we focus on is who we will become.* Fortunately, in life we can focus on more than one thing – but not too many.

If we put too many balls in the air, we become someone with too many balls in the air. "Jack of all trades, master of none" used to be an insult. In the global economy, it's a death sentence.

You can apply this further: whatever we focus on, we become experts in – though I prefer the word aficionado for expertise that has little or no chance of improving our lives. Before going to bed, I often watch bad movies on HBO or Cinemax. Therefore, I am becoming a bad movie aficionado. It is not affecting my livelihood, but it's not helping my livelihood either.

We all know people who hit happy hour every day. They are becoming happy hour experts (or aficionados by our definition). So it is that the Law of Accumulation can work for us or against us, or often, a bit of both. But if we want to change our economic destinies, we had better find a way to use this law to our advantage.

Not long ago, I was working on my laptop at the Northampton Brewery, putting the finishing touches on *Resumes From Hell*. A woman came up to me and belted out, "I've always wanted to write a book!" To which I replied: "Three hours a week for three years, and you'll have it."

It was not the answer she wanted to hear. We prefer to think of these things as beyond our reach. If it's impossible to accomplish dramatic things, then we can feel more secure in our rationalizations and save our best chances for the slot machines..

The Law of Accumulation is the enemy of rationalization. That's because applying the law doesn't require a lot of time, just consistency. Was it a pain in the posterior to write a book one day a week over three years? Sure. This new book is less graphic-intensive and should only take two years. Same deal: three hours a week. The Law of Accumulation says I will eventually be an author of many books. Will this solve all my problems? Not a chance. But will these published assets give me a chance to improve my life professionally and financially? That's a bet I'd be willing to make.

On some level, we all like to fantasize that we are in the process of becoming rock stars, business tycoons, and other persons of influence. The Law of Accumulation deflates these fantasies with a sharp taste of the truth. If we spend most of our time serving coffee, we are becoming baristas, and not much else. Perhaps the most bitter aspect: the things we focus on are not necessarily out of choice, but out of financial obligation.

Fortunately, we can counteract the trend of our dominant time commitment by initiating a counter-balancing, subordinate time commitment that develops a different theme. Eventually, a new theme matures to the point that it shifts our lives and brings on new and better opportunities.

"Developing themes" does get tedious. Most people would rather go snowboarding – so we have a culture of baristas who also happen to be snowboarding aficionados. Along those lines, some folks work jobs they can't stand in order to save for exotic vacations. You know the score: the Law dictates these folks are becoming people who have yucky jobs and go on nice vacations. Eventually, crummy jobs add up to a bad career. It becomes necessary to supplement the yearly escapes with Prozac or whisky shots or whatever else blurs the mirror.

For some, this is an acceptable tradeoff. But then again, if you were perfectly happy with your life, you wouldn't be reading this book. No worries: if you are OK with the tradeoffs of your life choices, you have little to fear from the Law of Accumulation. On the other hand, if you're like me, you are haunted by things not done and life not yet lived.

If you burn for more than what you've already been served, then you'd best take this law seriously. That means fighting for the time to develop an asset that may someday change your life. And yes, sometimes this means pushing away from the bar or the pool table or the fantasy football league. On the bright side, your projects will save you from a lot of yawner movie dates and tedious parties. Tough out the bad job if you must, but find a time or savings gap somewhere. Take less exotic vacations; claim the time and resources to finance a dream you don't want to sacrifice as the price of growing up.

Most good lives are structured by hard choices. But sometimes we give up *too much* because we think our window of opportunity has closed.

The Law of Accumulation (short for the Law of Accumulated Experience) says this isn't so. A few hours a week may be enough to develop the skills that could transform us. As for what to focus on, that's up to you; but if money is at the root of your problems, then be sure to choose something that passes my aficionado-versus-expert test.

According to this test, you can't become a balloon animal expert, only an aficionado. I'm not sure you can become a knitting expert, and I know for sure you can't become an expert on techno jams. Unless you see a financial connection, you're better off leaving those things in the recreational/hobby column and choosing another expertise to develop.

Make sure this expertise is something you can become world class at. And make sure it's experiential. By that I mean: pick something that's not just book-learning, but the applied learning of hands-on skills, shaped by the best information available.

Becoming a marketable expert is not the ultimate destination. It is only an intermediate phase, and it brings some traps of its own we'll cover in a bit. But becoming a sought-after expert *is* a significant step. The more you can make your mark as someone with unique know-how, the more you can dictate your own terms with the marketplace. Think of it as the end result of applied talent.

As an expert, you'll have a market value that allows you to take your skills to the best situation possible and not be held captive by one company. It's not easy to get there, but the Law of Accumulation can help you. And if you don't put it to work, it just might turn on you.

"Granted, the enforced savings of a mortgage payment is preferable to the blackjack table, but those who think that they are set for life because they've already funded an IRA or bought a home are not getting my point either."

What If You Don't Want to Start Your Own Business?

The best way to get rid of an idea is to put it in a box. The advantage to writing a book online (as this book was originally written) is that readers can misunderstand (or mock) your ideas 24/7 and let you know about it for good measure.

One misconception I've been hearing about: "this book is for business owners, so if you're not inclined to start your own business, then it has no relevance." That's a convenient way to box this book up, but I don't agree.

Earlier, I made the argument that the working world has been turned on its head, and that the real risk is putting faith in the 9 to 5 world. If this argument is correct, there is indeed a case for starting your own venture now, but let's put the idea of starting your own business aside and see if my argument has broader relevance.

Start with this book's basic assumption, that the global economy has impacts on the economic prospects of most modern workers, spreading from blue collar to white collar/"information economy" workers whose jobs are now vulnerable to outsourcing. There is a storehouse of statistics to support this point, but I'm going to leave it as a basic assumption and not get bogged down in stats here. If you disagree with this premise, you may have trouble with the conclusions I base on it. I will do my best to update my Web site, FreeFromCorporateAmerica.com, with some of this "supporting data" for those who are interested in it.

My next premise: something should be done about this. Not all agree. Some believe that as long as the economy grows, employment numbers will somehow find a way to keep up. But I meet more and more people who are bothered by a feeling that their economic fate is now out of their control. They'd like to go to work without wondering when the hammer is going to fall.

If you're with me so far, then there are two kinds of responses to these economic trends (and you don't have to choose between them).

One response is a political one: regardless of your political orientation, you could attempt to shift the economic discussion back to a focus on American jobs and/or corporate accountability. The problem is that martyrdom is too high a price for most folks to bear. Those that do step into that fray deserve our encouragement, but these trends are powerful enough to humble anyone who thinks they can change them before the next ice age, much less in time to pay the rent.

Most of us don't want to risk our careers for the sake of proving a point, so we need another option besides singling ourselves out as social change agents. Yes, we can still make our presence felt at the ballot box, but we're understandably reluctant to entrust elected officials with our job security. That's why the second kind of response – the one this book is concerned with – is a personal one.

The premise: "These trends may or may not end up hurting my future, but they seem to be permanent. There must be a way to feel more economically powerful and professionally secure. I want to have a lot more control over when, how, and for whom I work." That response is what this book is about.

Within the context of this personal response, there are a range of choices. At the extreme end: start your own business immediately. This is something only the most financially secure (or desperate) should consider. A less extreme response is to start a side business financed by your current employment. When the side business starts generating income, a transition to that business can be made. But starting a business (one way or the other) is just one possible response. It is *not* the only one.

The mindset we are after can be utilized even by someone who has dug into a long-term corporate career.

We are talking about two shifts here:

The first is a change in how to approach the "salaried employee" part of a career. Starting now, view your career as a series of proactive moves that you'll initiate in order to build your own skills and your own brand equity as much as your employer's. I'll cover this in more detail later.

The second shift: whether or not we are happy with our career prospects, we need to develop assets outside of the corporate basket. We need wealth of our own that is not tied to a company's goodwill towards us, or even to a 401k.

I have a friend who sold a screenplay for six figures. He didn't have his own company. He developed his asset (a screenplay) and found a broker – an agent in this case – to sell that asset for him. So it's possible to create assets that attain a market value without starting your own company.

Whether you rely on an outside broker or not, it's helpful to have a grasp of the sales and marketing side of things (more on this later also). Either way, you can adopt the "asset mentality" I am advocating without formally declaring yourself an entrepreneur. Bottom line? It sure feels a lot better in the Monday morning cubicle when you've spent part of your weekend putting a different economic iron – one that you own and control – into the fire.

With that, I hope we've laid to rest the perception that this book is only for those who want to start their own businesses. On the other hand, the narrow definition of "personal assets" most Americans buy into (build up your 401k, own your own home) is not what I am talking about either.

Granted, the enforced savings of a mortgage payment is preferable to the blackjack table, but those who think they are set for life because they've already funded an IRA or bought a home are not getting my point either. We'll need more than pink flamingos on our lawns to have a chance at real autonomy.

I'll take more swipes at 401ks and home ownership shortly, so pretty soon you'll have a better idea of why I see these "assets" as insufficient. An effective personal response to the global economy requires a different approach to careers *and* asset management. It may or may not mean opening your own business. It *will* mean thinking like an owner. Thinking like an employee means working for people who don't have your best interests at heart.

Ownership as a concept makes obvious sense, and not just because the deck is stacked for owners in this economic system. I use the word in a broader sense. Ownership, to me, implies taking full responsibility for your life, claiming the upside of who you can become, and enduring the risk that is required to have a shot at a life beyond ordinary.

"The folks we're concerned with here face a different kind of danger: they think they are set for life, when in fact their financial fate is precarious."

Gut Check #1: Where We Are and What's Next

Those who are not persuaded may never be. Those who *are* have work to do. Developing assets is time consuming, so it may be time to set this book down and do it. There are more tips to share on the asset development stage, but they mostly pertain to getting through the inevitable rough patches. See the concluding section of this book for more on handling adversity. For now, the key is to head to the lab and come out with something you want to market.

After the asset is obtained, next comes the issue of how to bring those assets to market, and how to make the most of the time you *do* spend in corporate environments. We'll get to those topics soon. At this point, I'm going to assume that the readership is now divided between those who are fired up to give this a shot and those who aren't sold yet. There may be a few sitting on the fence. If you fit that bill, the next few chapters could be especially provocative.

The things I'm going to hammer away at next might seem odd. People fall into a false comfort zone because they think one of three assets is going to take care of them: their home, their 401k, or their career snapshot, otherwise known as a resume. (I could probably throw in wealthy spouses and/or kids who can dunk a basketball, but I'm not going there.)

Some of you may wonder why I am picking on these "assets" when they are a much better use of money and time than addictive vices.

Those who are scraping the bottom tend to know exactly where they are; they don't delude themselves into a false comfort zone. But others face a different kind of danger: they think they are set for life (or at least heading in that direction), when in fact their financial fate is precarious. The Enron employees who lost their 401ks are the poster children, but since Enron, we've seen countless other examples.

Despite these 401k meltdowns, I still see too many people who think they are secure because they have money sunk into what I call "false assets." So that's where we're headed next.

Part IV:

False Assets

Home Is Not (Necessarily) an Asset

The Problem with 401ks (and IRAs)

Hard Work Is Overrated

Burn Your Resume

Graduating Into Nothing –
Degrees Are Not the Best Credentials

Gut Check #2: From "Somebody's Employee" to
Sought-After Expert

"Lots of folks love the Home Depot weekend: buy some stuff you may or may not need, spend the weekend puttering around. This may be a fun lifestyle, but I wouldn't rationalize it by saying, 'We're increasing the value of our home.' The wallpaper that goes up in the den will be stripped out by the next buyer."

Home Is Not (Necessarily) an Asset

Home ownership is not all it's cracked up to be. So why do financial advisors roll it out as the best move for those who want to improve their finances? Mostly because home ownership is an excellent form of enforced savings. No one wants the sheriff to set their fridge on the lawn, so people move mountains to get that mortgage payment in.

I don't have a problem with home ownership. I *do* have a problem with people listing their homes in the asset column and assuming they are in good shape financially. Homes are an asset, no doubt about that, but there is a huge difference between an asset we live in and a rental property we own. A rental property is an asset with a capital A. A home is an asset with a lowercase a.

We do all kinds of things to our homes which may or may not help their market value. We put a pool in and justify it as an asset. When we try to sell that home, buyers see a big lawsuit in the ground.

True, there are improvements that almost always increase a home's value: a revamped kitchen, a new master bedroom.

Home ownership *can* be a step in the right fiscal direction, or it can be a huge drain of time and energy.

Lots of folks love the Home Depot weekend: buy some stuff you may or may not need, spend the weekend puttering around. This may be a fun lifestyle, but I wouldn't rationalize it by saying, "We're increasing the value of our home." The wallpaper going up in the den will be stripped out by the next buyer.

People tend to upgrade with each home they buy. Trading up may lead to a better lifestyle, but it also means there is less cashing out on the appreciation than we might think. Often, homeowners don't see the benefit of trading up until the nest empties and the big place is downsized.

I'll concede this much: home ownership *can* prevent some worst case scenarios. When you get stuck, you can borrow against the value of a home, and home equity lines tend to be superior to credit card interest rates. But in this book, we'll take a skeptical view of home ownership as an asset. It only qualifies to be our asset-in-development if it meets certain additional criteria.

To call a home an asset, it must be approached as an investment, with the same analytical disinterest we apply to our other investment holdings. That means our residence can rarely be called an asset. It's hard to separate emotional considerations when it comes to the home we live in. I know successful real estate investors who got their start by moving into homes, fixing and "flipping" them, but most folks don't feel like boxing up their lives every year or two.

Many have gotten rich off real estate appreciation, but beware the "click your heels and wait for the value to go up" mentality. The appreciation of real estate is not a given, as the current housing bubble just demonstrated.

So how can a home become an asset? Start by making good on the first principle of business: buy low, sell high. Good real estate investing comes down to a simple question: how much did you pay for it? You have to know your neighborhood and the cost of time and materials for the fix-ups. You have to know which enhancements are marketable and what the red tape is (inspections and building regulations) in your area. And if you find a home outside your price parameters, no matter how much you covet it, you cannot buy. Not if you want to call it an asset.

If you have the skills to fix up your home yourself, that's yet another way you can add value to the price you paid. The more you have to outsource the improvements to specialists either due to lack of time or the regulations in your area for trade work (electrical, plumbing), the harder it is to make money through rehab.

Unless you live in a lucky area where home prices are surging and you're locked in; the way to succeed in real estate is by approaching it as a true business. And that means investing in something besides the home you live in. For those who focus on a specialized aspect of real estate (new construction, foreclosures, buy/fix/flip), it can be one of the best side businesses you can start.

The upside is high, and the risk is buffered by the underlying asset. If it's hard to increase the value of a home, it's even harder to wreck it – though I understand the artist once again known as Prince was recently sued by NBA player Carlos Boozer for "Princifying" one of Boozer's homes.

Sometimes it's a disadvantage to invest in other properties when you own your own home (it may initially limit your purchasing power on investment properties), but this can be overcome. The main thing is to make sure that the time you spend on your own home doesn't suck up the time you would have spent on your investment strategy.

My company would not be in business today without two buy/fix/sell properties I turned around in Boston in the late

90s with the help of a business partner on the construction side. One key thing to remember: real estate is not a very liquid asset. Until you own a bunch of properties and can leverage one against the other, it's easy to run into a cash flow pinch.

At one point during our rehab projects, I almost lost my job. I had to take a pay cut and carry $5,000 a month in mortgage payments on credit cards. While I was carrying those mortgages, I found myself in a work situation I really needed to walk away from. But I could not afford to lose that job until the homes were sold, so I sucked it up and endured one of the most ludicrous years of my life. It was probably the right decision, but I was dogged by a feeling of self-betrayal.

Whether you are improving your own home or buying rental properties, make sure the real estate business suits you. I've already written about why I currently focus on books instead of real estate, even though real estate is the better investment: my passion lies elsewhere.

Life is too short to focus on side ventures we don't love. Our work lives are already filled with projects we have misgivings about. Anything we start on the side needs to lean more towards labor of love than grudging responsibility. We can (and should) take the marketplace into account when we choose our projects, but not to the point where we have tenants with broken water heaters taking us away from writing the next great American novel.

"Should we really pin our hopes on the smiling faces of the discount brokers who profit from each transaction while offering us reassuring advice about historical rates of return"?

The Problem With 401ks (and IRAs)

If you make decent money and have absolutely no self-control, 401ks are great. Otherwise, I'd take a more skeptical view. It all depends: if you're happy socking money away in order to live the good life when you're too old to enjoy it, then a 401k/retirement account mentality is perfect. But if you'd like to see the mountaintop before you're too creaky to climb it without the help of a chair lift, then you should consider the downsides of the 401k.

Let's put the critique of the 401k in the context of this book. First, I don't consider a 401k as our asset-in-development because it's just not liquid enough. Despite exceptions like the first-time homebuyer's allowance, the penalties for early withdrawal are typically prohibitive. A 401k can fit into the overall financial picture nicely, but it rarely deserves to be put in the center.

Employers are less likely to offer comprehensive stock plans these days. We've seen enough people lose shirts to know that a good 401k should have way more than one company's stock in it anyway. If you plan to have a retirement account as part of your strategy, I would suggest an asset allocation approach.

"Asset allocation" simply means that your portfolio will be broad enough to shield you from down markets. Studies of asset allocation have shown that a diversity of investment holdings protects from worst case scenarios while providing a good upside.

To me, a good retirement account goes beyond stocks and bonds to include other asset classes such as real estate funds and even some precious metals. International investments are also a piece of the puzzle, and of course it should all be tailored to match your age and risk tolerance level.

A well-balanced 401k is nice because it doesn't require fretting and fussing. A sudden market dip won't hurt a diversified portfolio nearly as much. Obviously there are reams of books on this topic, so you're probably more interested in hearing why I have issues with 401ks and IRAs.

Beyond the liquidity problem, the next problem is that IRAs violate our law of focus. The most valuable assets are the ones we focus on. Most folks with retirement accounts are not exactly market experts. We're lucky if we understand the investment philosophy of the funds we put our fate in. Most people's portfolios are a mixture of blind faith and infatuation picks like technology stocks.

I like real estate better. When you buy a property, you are in on the ground floor of an investment. By the time you invest in a stock, it's already been through an initial public offering (IPO). Early stage investors have already made their millions and gotten out. I suppose the same is true in real estate, but no one is stopping us from buying a piece of land and building something of value. Getting in on an IPO is another matter entirely.

You can make a go of the stock market as your asset of choice *if* you make it a focus. I still remember my grandfather huddled over the stock listings at the crack of dawn clutching a big magnifying glass. I couldn't have swung my college tuition without his stock market mornings. But he put in the hours. He understood the companies and industries he invested in; he knew the philosophy of the management teams. He did everything but visit those companies and kick tires. How many of us can say the same? Is it smart to put a crucial part of our savings into investments we don't monitor carefully and don't know a heck of a lot about?

Investment gurus will cry foul, pointing to the rates of return that stocks have typically provided, which do appear better than stashing money under a pillow. But who wants to be part of an historical oddity? What if we're living in an era that turns out to be the exception to the historical average?

A case could be made that global conditions, such as the surge in the Chinese and Indian economies and the declining power of the dollar – not to mention the increased scarcity of natural resources – could create, at best, a volatile investment climate, and at worst, a significant market crisis. (Note: this chapter, as well as the real estate chapter, were written well ahead of the crisis that has now arrived.)

Should we really pin our hopes on the smiling faces of the discount brokers who profit from each of our transactions while offering reassuring advice about "historical rates of return"? Sure, there are always good buys if you can crystal ball which bottom-feeders are going to turn around, but that sport can prove frustrating. I subscribe to the argument that overall, most U.S. stocks worth owning are either over-valued or fairly-valued. The average price-to-earnings ratio of NYSE stocks supports my argument, and you can't get the true benefit of the rare "ten baggers," those portfolio-saving stocks that double in size more than ten times over, through the comparative safety of a mutual fund. The biggest gains are made by picking individual winners yourself, and that's where the homework comes in.

Even if you do OK, there is an opportunity cost to stock investing: you could be using that same cash to develop assets you have more control over. Why not pour money into our own ventures as opposed to some water cooler stock pick? By the time most of us reach retirement age, water is going to cost $5 a bottle. How that will affect the stock market is anyone's guess, but I wouldn't put all my eggs in that basket.

Strangely enough, the most dangerous thing about 401ks is that they are tax-protected, so the temptation to shelter pre-tax income in these vehicles can be overwhelming. The paranoid desire to avoid taxes is not part of a sound financial strategy. Putting money into a tax-free IRA can be problematic from a cash flow standpoint.

A cautionary tale from my own amateur investments: in the mid-90s, I was making the best salary of my life. I thought I was a business genius, but it turns out the forgiving dotcom economy was the true source of my largesse. Cash flowed – it wasn't hard to sock a bunch of money into tax-protected mutual funds.

When I went online and saw my retirement fund in six figures, I thought I was a pretty cool guy. I had a vague feeling that a lot of my mutual funds were overvalued. Since everything I invested in went up, I didn't trouble myself. But when the bubble burst, I lost about 70 percent of those holdings. It was only a decent level of asset allocation that saved me from losing even more.

After that debacle, I left that company and started my own. Cash was at a premium. Money made from real estate holdings got me off the ground, but to get through the post-9/11 years, I had to liquidate what was left of my retirement account and endure a sizeable penalty.

Looking back, there's no question in my mind that I should have avoided 401ks, taken a tax hit on all my income, and stockpiled cash. Some of that cash would have been an emergency fund; the rest would have gone into real estate and maybe into my books. During those years, my construction partner in Maine found some waterfront land we might have bought that ended up going up in value at least six times. It's not an exaggeration to say there was a million-dollar upside to some of the land deals we saw. But we did not have the resources to get in.

I'm not complaining; I would not have a business today without the two real estate projects we *did* complete. Yes, I took a big tax hit on those profits. But the end result was cash I have access to now, earned from investments I understood in an industry I was comfortable in.

We had a relationship with a realtor who knew every pot-hole in a particular Boston neighborhood; she led us to two great properties we bought at the right price. I've never had that kind of inside track on any stock. And with real estate, there are ways of legally shielding money from taxes as well, such as rolling the profits from a sale into another property.

A 401k fits the classic model of "work hard, save, and retire." But I wonder if that mindset fits the workplace we find ourselves in now. 401ks are *not* a bad idea. If you're aware of the risks, and you still have money on the side to develop other assets, then by all means, use the 401k as a piece of your financial strategy. But if the money going into your 401k is preventing you from investing in yourself, take a harder look. Mastering one industry is enough of a challenge. There's something to be said for only buying into things we understand.

"Meantime, while I was being such a productive guy, a couple of nose-picking computer geeks slept in, put on their bunny slippers, and bought up some URL addresses."

Hard Work Is Overrated

You can't go a day without hearing someone get teary-eyed about the virtues of hard work. As someone who has worked as hard as anyone with a questionable life to show for it, I am here to prove that hard work is overrated. The "work smarter, not harder" crowd has the upper hand. Most of us were huddled over hard work while our greatest opportunities passed us by. We were too busy paying our dues to notice.

Take an extreme example from the dotcom economy: in the mid-90s, I was working hard to establish myself as a technical recruiter. I knew all about the Internet and how it was changing the job economy. So I went about the business of making as many job placements as possible. Since placements averaged $20,000 and I had a fifty-percent commission percentage on the deals I closed, I wasn't complaining.

But I was thinking small. You don't settle for a handful of nuggets in the midst of a gold rush. I worked until the wee hours. I had so many voice mails, I wrote them on paper squares and taped them to my window shade until it made wallpaper. I returned calls into the evening, doing my best to get to them all.

Meantime, while I was being such a productive guy, a couple of nose-picking computer geeks slept in, put on their bunny slippers, and bought up URL addresses like business.com. Then they chilled out, held onto those URLs for a year or two, and sold them for millions. I worked harder, they worked less, and they got a lot more back. That's because the economy is structured to reward ownership, not sweat.

People have a hard time letting go of the ideal of hard work because they want to believe in some kind of meritocracy where those who bust their butt get their eventual day in the sun. That's a wrong-headed, naïve way to look at life. Here's a better analogy: think of hard work as the accelerator and business strategy as the steering wheel. If you're heading in the wrong direction, working harder just smacks you into the wall sooner.

In the early 90s, there was a club around here called the Bay State Hotel where the local music legends had their day. There was a bartender down there who was a double-shifter to the core. He worked days at a deli and nights closing the bar. I'd never met someone so bitter and worn down. He was a relentless work zombie; I was in awe of his work ethic.

Contrast this to another fellow I knew back then who had a sizable ownership interest in a computer company. This guy hated to work. He was the kind of insufferable owner who comes in once a week, criticizes some people, messes up some good ideas, and heads out again. He lived in the woods and drew a nice salary while dragging his company like a car boot.

The company became very successful in spite of him. Eventually, they needed to get rid of him in order to have the authority to make decisions on being acquired. This guy ended up getting paid a hefty sum to go away. Nobody in the company worked less than him, but he got paid for being a jerk. The contrast between this fellow and the double-shift bartender taught me everything I needed to know about hard work.

I'll be the first to stand up for the importance of discipline and consistency when it comes to reaching goals. But strategy comes first. I've been dismayed to see that my determination to go the extra mile has actually backfired, leading me to states of physical exhaustion that are too terrifying to be proud of. It's better to accept that we have human limitations. Don't try to find out what those limitations are.

The goal of this chapter is two-fold: first, to scare workaholics into realizing that accumulating massive timesheets is not a wise approach to wealth creation. Second, to encourage those who are considering developing assets of your own to give it a shot. Quit trying to outwork everyone in your office; back off from your day job if you have to. Make sure to get time in on your own ventures.

I'm certainly not advocating a careless approach to work. I've been amazed by opportunities friends have scored by investing passion into ridiculously dull jobs. After graduating, one of my best friends moved from scanning bar codes at a computer gaming store in the mall to managing a computer consulting business – all because one of his customers liked his attitude. In some cases, pride in your work can take you a long way. Attitude can definitely lead to opportunity. But there are predicaments you can't employee your way out of.

I measure my side projects by two criteria: profitability and the extent of my own involvement. The second distinction is vital: if I have a venture that is profitable, but costs a great deal of my time and energy, then I mark it as a project to re-evaluate when finances are better. On the other hand, if I develop an asset that generates income with little or no involvement from me, then I follow that model and develop more of the same.

Right now, my most efficient asset is my SAP consulting book. I'm not making a whole lot of money on it, no more than a thousand dollars a month in profit, but I haven't worked hard on book promotion in years. I *do* make a point of keeping myself visible on SAP Web sites, but it is not a big time commitment.

When you type in the keyword "SAP" into Amazon, my book is likely to come out near the top of the listings. In business terms, that is a "virtuous circle." It took me several years to get the book to that point, but now, without my continued efforts, the Amazon search rankings are continuously generating new sales. Google also lists the book prominently on a couple of popular SAP search phrases.

Obviously, the efficiency of this small-scale success has my attention. I am now writing a follow up SAP book, and of course I am finishing this one. I am pursuing a business strategy that rewards the least effort possible. I am *not* looking for reasons to slack off – I'm looking to make enough money to buy the time to pursue bigger dreams. I have a long way to go, but I have a lot better strategy than I used to.

I can hear the rebuttal: "When you develop assets on the side, aren't you actually working *harder* than before?" To a degree, that is true. There are certainly times when I would rather do something besides slug away at this book. My clients certainly aren't cutting me a break on deadlines because I have a neato writing project underway.

But here's what's interesting: by making time for this book, I also do a better job of protecting my time and making better decisions on how I spend it. Yes, there are still times where I space out for a few hours watching bad movies and ask myself, "Now why did you do that?" But for the most part, my books give me a focus I wouldn't otherwise have.

Most of us give way too much time to our employers. It comes from the best of intentions. We have high standards for our work; we hope our dues-paying adds up to some kind of karmic reward, or heck, at least a promotion. But folks who pay crazy dues pack up their desks like everyone else when the pink slips come. Perhaps that all-nighter at the office won't add up to much after all. Shaving off an hour here or there might be all we need to get our own projects off the ground.

Yes, the time crunch of developing an asset while working full time gets tight. But remind yourself: which time commitment has the greater upside? This book has been time-consuming, but the upside of publishing it is so much greater than the three hours a week I spend.

It's a wakeup call to realize that our grandfathers' lunchpail-to-work mentality is self-defeating. But especially in corporate circles, we must be wary of giving too much time to things we do not own and control.

I could pack an entire book with the disappointments of friends and colleagues who gave their all to companies that now exist only on rarely-worn visors and stiff t-shirts. In some cases, those companies went bankrupt. In tougher-to-swallow situations, the owners cashed out and left employees with nothing – unless you count a "thanks for all you've done" handshake.

But handshakes don't pay the bills. Hard work for slick people is usually a bad idea. And for those of you who can't conceive of getting up in the morning without some arduous leaf-raking, don't worry, any asset we develop is going to involve some good old-fashioned hard work before it's done.

But if we choose the right undertaking, not only will we have a better chance of making out financially, we'll experience the most fulfilling work of all: the joy of working on projects we truly care about, alongside people we respect and enjoy. And that may be the one thing more important than a paycheck.

"The most successful people in the world don't need resumes. They don't have to pee in a cup and take personality compatibility tests."

Burn Your Resume

It's pretty hypocritical for someone who wrote a book on resumes to advocate burning them. But wait, it gets worse: I'm writing another one. I've even given workshops on resume "do's and don'ts" where I talk about the rules of the job search game.

I do this work for one reason: if people spent as much time marketing their skills as they did acquiring them, they'd be better off. At its best, the resume can present your skills in a compelling light and serve as a door-opener.

But mastering the resume only gets you so far. You can be a pro at the employment game and still get trapped in pink slip culture, forever chasing jobs with companies that hire and fire with impunity. Credentials don't make you impervious to setbacks.

When the Information Technology job market collapsed after Y2K, the higher-level managers drew the shortest straw. Sure, programmers took pay cuts, and many were forced into new fields. But for managers (the ones with the sterling resumes), switching fields was not an option. They had invested too much time in their career path. You could understand why they didn't want to dust off a desk and start fishing for real estate listings alongside entry-level salespeople.

Resumes are a passport through a problematic job market. But if our skills are dependent on employment by an outside institution, even with a well-stocked resume, our options are limited. Consider the case of a CIO (Chief Information Officer). The job title sounds pretty nifty, but only certain companies have such a position. "CIO" looks great on resumes, but if your company sends you packing without notice, you could ride the pine for three to six months until something else comes along.

I'm not recommending that we hover in a state of professional mediocrity to avoid getting caught too high up the ladder. But the most successful people in the world don't need resumes. They don't have to pee in a cup and take personality compatibility tests.

So how do we get there? By now, you know my answer: we get there by developing income-producing assets of our own – things that might not even go on our resumes because we don't want to intimidate our next employer. But we should always have a side project going that could take us to the promised land. Or if not to the promised land, then at least to "just say no," a pretty cool place where you have the economic clout to say "no!" to any employer that crosses the line.

Most people don't have the power to say no to our employers, no matter how irritating or demanding they might be. We are deer-in-headlights when management corners us with the good ol', "Yeah, I'm going to need you to go ahead and come in on Saturday and finish up those TPS reports." Understandably so – you can't draw lines in the sand unless you are prepared to walk.

Developing an asset mentality means we are investing in our own dignity – not necessarily so we can stick a middle finger in our boss's face, but so we can negotiate more favorable terms on any job we agree to.

For most managers, it's second nature to wring the last drop of productivity from those who work for them. But here's where it gets interesting: when you have the strength (and options) to push back, you'll be surprised how many managers not only respond to that kind of firmness, but actually respect you more for not taking their guff – especially if you can show them how you can make a more powerful contribution with fewer sticky notes on your desk.

The other day, I updated my resume. It's a habit I can't seem to kick. But I look forward to the day when I can pile 'em and burn 'em. So what about the hypocrisy of writing books on resumes and then mocking their value? Even if you plan on inventing a new game, you still have to master the current one. Learning how to promote yourself in the existing job market goes hand in hand with developing assets on the side. One relates to current cash flow needs, the other to longer-term solutions.

Now that I've poked holes in 401ks, home ownership, and resumes, the end result should be a better argument for the importance of an "asset mentality." The goal was not to scare people, but to point out that the things most of us fall back on aren't going to provide a very soft landing.

There's more: we need to look at how to take our assets to market, and we also need tactics for dealing with the adversity we will face. But before we go there, a hard look at the value of formal education is in order.

"The best way to avoid grinding beans is to learn how to sell them. If you think school can teach you how to do that, you've probably had too much schooling."

Graduating Into Nothing – Degrees Are Not the Best Credentials

An undergraduate degree is no shelter from the storm. Sure, a bachelor's degree impacts your salary over a lifetime. But the service industry is littered with waitresses, bellhops and even a few grocery baggers who are not overly impressed with the earning power of their degrees.

I'm not going to waste time on the merits of an undergrad degree; even a basher like me has to admit: a degree helps more than it hurts. No, it doesn't guarantee you won't serve spicy fries, but a bachelor's degree is a career insurance policy. You won't be blocked from an opportunity because you don't have one.

And what if you do end up in school? Should you study what you are passionate about, or what ensures your future marketability? Should you approach education as an intellectual challenge or as trade school? I'm not going to settle that worthy argument. But I will say that learning how to market your passions is a much better idea than shelving your passions for commerce.

Let's say we (reluctantly) accept the four-year degree as the prudent move. Then we face a more important question: what about advanced degrees? Most undergrads look to graduate school as a family-funded parachute over the taco-stained terrain of the service industry. Can't blame them: as one recent graduate from a very prestigious college said to me, "A college degree feels more like a high school diploma these days." A degree may land you a job, but not necessarily a good one, unless your dream job is restraining violent adolescents. Most graduates land in the working world with a thud and don't like their prospects. The first impulse is to jump right back into school, and that's the impulse we're going to take issue with here.

Graduate schools are havens for people who didn't have the guts to pursue their entrepreneurial dreams. Others are there to avoid disappointing their families. The problem is that graduate school only pans out if you are there to pursue a burning ambition that you cannot achieve another way. There's nothing quite so foul as getting stuck in a career you didn't want with a degree you no longer want because your family offered conditional support – *if* you took the path of most credentials.

That's one good thing about degrees: the more you have, the more likely you are to be trotted out like a show pony at family functions. Of course, some folks are in grad school because they are in pursuit of their life's work, and those people are to be respected. But when you go to school because you think an extra degree is going to save you from grinding coffee beans, you may be on the wrong track.

The best way to avoid grinding beans is to learn how to sell them. If you think school can teach you how to do that, you've probably had too much schooling. In business, you either learn to cut deals or you get used to hearing about them afterwards. Since deals have a lot to do with relationships, every year you spend inside a classroom impressing your relatives is one less year you have to cultivate the connections (and take the humbling knocks) that are behind what we call "success."

Six years out of college, I visited a family friend who was knee deep in medical school. When he learned how much money I was making and then met my girlfriend, he flipped out. He was busting his ass with no social life. The only reason he was in med school was to someday make the kind of money I was already making so that he might someday date the kind of woman I was already dating. Years later, he dropped out of medical school in a daze of debt and regrets, and with a pharmaceutical drug addiction to boot. He was in the game for the wrong reasons.

If your game is making money, an advanced degree is not required. It may even be a detriment. Much of what we learn in school has no bearing on professional success. Obviously scientists need PhDs, lawyers need JDs, ministers need MDivs. The same goes for the trades, from electrical to acupuncture.

Otherwise, advanced degrees can be dangerous. PhDs can even be a hindrance to finding work in other fields; small minds get intimidated by excess credentials. You may be wondering how I feel about MBAs. They are vital to high-level executive careers, less so for anything else – *as long as you are willing to put in the time and learn as you go.*

The more lacking you are in self-discipline, the more useful school is. But if you can master the art of self-education, you don't need to depend on formal schooling. Whenever you pursue ambitious goals, whether it's parenting or investing or sailing, there is a role for specialized knowledge. The best way to acquire that is in the trenches.

Each week in business, something happens that underscores what I don't know. Recently I found myself on the ignorant end of a business dealing which showed me I don't know enough about global economic trends, so now I'm listening to a series of audiotapes on economics.

This kind of self-education should be integrated into our lives. It's far more affordable (and effective) to learn this way, but the catch is that you have to turn off *Californication* and fire up the DVD lecture series. If that sounds like hell on earth, then the structure of school might be a better option. There is always adult education, which is a happy medium between a full-time degree program and education on-the-fly.

If you don't think through this on the front end, you can end up with some pretty expensive trophies. I know a local artist who has a PhD he doesn't use. His real love is painting. Yet he has an advanced degree he worked hard for; he feels the need to use it. More than a few times, he's come to me for advice on "what's next," even though I haven't set foot in a grad school classroom.

Granted, he's pretty stupid to come to me for help, but the fact that he is desperate enough to do so doesn't inspire confidence. He doesn't need his PhD to paint, and he definitely doesn't need it to serve gin and tonics. As someone looking over my shoulder while I was writing said, "We need to become savvy consumers of our own education in America."

Agreed. That includes understanding the limitations of formal schooling at any level.

The four areas of knowledge most essential to adult happiness are: financial mastery, emotional intelligence, spiritual development, and physical well-being. This book is concerned with financial mastery; I'm not going to lose focus by elaborating on the other three, except to acknowledge that without all four, success will remain elusive.

In case I have thrown around too many catch phrases without defining them, I view "emotional intelligence" as mastery of interpersonal relationships. "Spiritual development" is the hardest of the four to describe easily, but for this book's purposes, let's consider it a balance between self-knowledge and some type of broader understanding of how we fit into the bigger picture, and especially, where we turn to for solace.

As for "physical well-being," this may seem so utterly obvious that it's silly to name it as a necessary part of our self-education. But navigating the health care system takes plenty of skill – not to mention the challenge of staying in good physical condition instead of becoming a bloated cubicle accessory. For most of us, physical well-being requires as much intentional effort as the other three aspects of adult happiness.

Success in these four areas is not something that is accomplished casually; you have to actively seek out the right knowledge and put it into practice. Yet I know of few schools that address these areas in the context of their core curriculum. We run the risk of becoming intellectually unbalanced – well versed in esoteric areas but lacking in crucial skills.

In high school, I spent more time memorizing the rivers in Oklahoma than I did learning how to write a resume. In college, I spent more time critiquing our economic system than learning how to succeed within it. What we *do* learn in school is not meaningless, but if we want to master the aspects of life that are central to our happiness and autonomy, we're going to have to teach ourselves something.

The time we put into acquiring advanced degrees may rob us of the chance to master things that are more relevant to the real bottom line of our own happiness. As someone who comes from a family lineage of dysfunctional PhDs, I can state with authority that the phenomenon of the miserable well-stocked mind is alive and well.

The process of asset creation *does* involve tackling new fields, and new fields are best conquered through the ongoing integration of theory and practice. Self-education plays a hugely important role, but formal degrees are not the only way through the turnstile. Starting your own company doesn't even require a bachelor's degree. Still, I think it's worth sucking it up and getting that much behind you sooner rather than later. Beyond undergrad, all bets are off.

Degrees should be pursued when they are the one obstacle in the way of our best livelihood. Otherwise, we're better off in the beautiful uncertainty of the garage, tinkering around with computer parts alongside the ghosts of young Steve Jobs and Bill Gates. In the end, the best credentials are the ones we make out of our accomplishments.

"We don't want to rub our eyes each morning resenting our work and viewing it as an obstacle in the way of a better livelihood. Is there a way to change that around?"

Gut Check #2: From "Somebody's Employee" to Sought-After Expert

So where are we? We've taken a hard look at "false assets." We've examined the limitations of education and careerism and shown how they underscore the need for an asset mentality. A methodology for creating assets on the side has already been established, one that can be followed whether or not we start our own business.

As much as possible, our strategy has taken into account that most people are already way too busy and maybe even a little overwhelmed by their current circumstances.

What's next? For most of us, it's a dual track: on the one hand, we're actively plotting our side ventures. But usually we also have our current jobs to contend with, many of them in a corporate context. How can we get the most out of those situations instead of just punching the clock? We don't want to rub our eyes each morning resenting work as an obstacle in the way of a better life. Is there a way to change that around?

The next section on "making the shift" talks about how to address that through an emphasis on self-branding, as well as developing a marketable expertise that provides you with more options and opportunities. By shifting the focus to your own name brand and reputation, you'll create a market position that is less tied to one employer.

Pulling this off means doing counter-intuitive things sometimes, such as turning down corner offices in favor of practical skills that have broader relevance. In today's workplace, marketability is about acquiring skills, not fancy job titles. It's about becoming an expert with visibility beyond your company.

The next section talks about how to move ahead with that objective, while pointing out that the cult of the expert has some problems of its own that we need to anticipate.

Of course, as we've noted, being dependent on outside institutions for employment is a flawed approach in the context of a global labor pool. That's where our other track comes in. As we're shifting our attitudes about how we work for others, we're also building our own assets on the side. Once we do that, we can move those assets into the marketplace. And that's where it gets a little tricky for those of us who are not exactly comfortable with finance, sales and marketing. We'll pick up on those topics after the next section.

Part V:

Making the Shift: Brand Yourself as an Expert

Don't Brand Your Employer, Brand Yourself

Chase Skills, Not Dollars
(and Management Is for Suckers)

Moving Beyond the Cult of the Expert

Gut Check #3: From the Lab to the Marketplace

"Companies have a clever way of getting employees to work selflessly on their behalf. By the time you wise up, there's another bright-eyed youngster only too eager to carry the corporate torch."

Don't Brand Your Employer, Brand Yourself

The battle for the consumer now starts in the mind. The horrifying conclusion: companies want you to see their brand everywhere. These days, companies put a higher value on their brand than their physical assets. The smug term for this? "Brand equity." Brand equity implies that consumers who have seen enough ads for your sports drink will compulsively reach for it.

Branding can be very irritating, especially to those of us who would rather see a greasy local diner than a McDonald's arch (I asked Burger King if they wanted to sponsor this sentence but they declined). But while we might not like being hounded by brands, we can't quarrel with their effectiveness.

There is definitely a relationship between how often we see a brand and how often we buy it. Brandidentityguru.com puts it a little more diabolically: "Customers factor brands into every purchase. The stronger the brand, meaning the clearer the position it occupies in their minds, the more value it has and the more likely they are to choose it – again and again."

Don't fight the branding trend; use it for your own purposes. When you work for a brand-conscious company, the first impulse is to devote yourself to pushing their brand so that you can score internal points. Hopefully those points can be cashed in for promotions and bonuses. But scoring points won't necessarily save you from pink slips. Employers have a clever way of getting people to work selflessly on the their behalf. By the time you wise up, there's another bright-eyed youngster only too eager to carry the corporate torch.

Even while you're working as an employee, you can often use your company to brand yourself. This personal branding can be a lifesaver when things go awry. Your brand is essentially a broadcasted version of your business reputation, a way for you to be visible beyond your present employer and known by others in your field. Companies want to frame things in terms of themselves, but in the process, they may end up branding you. Look for opportunities to have your name associated with outwardly-visible products and projects.

My biggest 90s employer spent a lot of money positioning themselves in the SAP market, but they also branded me as an SAP career expert. This visibility led to a book-writing opportunity and many future clients. When things turned sour with that employer, I had industry recognition to fall back on.

Being known in my field has generally forced people to be nicer to me and exploit me a little less. In reality, I didn't always have that many options, but my public visibility implied that I did, and perception makes all the difference. In that sense, branding is the process of perception becoming reality.

One proven branding tactic is to volunteer your time and expertise to outside groups. When you donate your time, you tend to be paid in visibility. Your current employer will often approve of this outside activity – as long as they are getting exposure as well. I write for other SAP Web sites as a way of getting more exposure; I make sure my clients benefit by listing their URLs in my bio and referring to their services when appropriate. Keeping your own brand alive is one of the smartest things you can do. If you can make yourself visible in an important field, the money will follow more often than not.

Another way you can enhance your brand name is by participating in online forums for your industry and putting up profiles on business networking sites like LinkedIn. Cultivating a business network, especially one that combines online and "in person" events like trade shows, can have a huge impact on your personal brand.

An extreme example of how corporate branding helps the individual: celebrity book deals. Mike Greenberg (of the sports radio show "Mike and Mike in the Morning") recently wrote a big bestseller, mostly cute stuff about being a sports broadcasting dad. ESPN has spent a lot of money boosting "Mike and Mike," and it led "Greenie" to a book deal, which ESPN continues to promote since it benefits their show's ratings and their network as a whole. Mike Greenburg's career is on very solid ground, and it's all because his own brand was inevitably promoted along with his employer's.

So is a well-established "personal brand" an asset by this book's definition? Almost. Name recognition can certainly lead directly to income. The catch is that most of those opportunities involve billing time as an expert. And as we'll get to shortly, joining the cult of the expert poses its own dangers.

Building your own brand is still one of the best moves you can make. It's a big step toward changing your economic terms of engagement. It's also a great way to get a handle on the brass tacks of marketing – skills that you will need as you develop (and brand) assets of your own.

There's one disclaimer I want to make about self-branding. Before you go about your branding project, just make sure that the area you choose is one you truly want to become an expert in. Maintaining expertise is a haul. If that expertise is not fueled by real vocational passion, you may end up regretting the professional bed you made.

Most of us do need a marketable trade that can get us through until our income-generating assets change the equation on how much we need to work. But we make one of two mistakes: either we choose a trade we love that is not marketable, or we force ourselves into a lucrative profession we have no desire to excel in.

So before the self-branding exercise begins, it's good to find the most marketable profession that taps into our core interests. Too often, we dismiss our talents instead of repositioning them. I've talked about how this works in the music business.

I've seen struggling musicians stay in the industry by getting on the other side of the studio glass or by becoming professional songwriters. These options wouldn't appeal to everyone, but before we permanently place our passions in the hobby column, we owe it to ourselves to see if we can turn them into our "transitional trade."

There's no knowing how long we're going to be working in that transitional phase before our assets-on-the-side kick in, so we need to choose a profession that will have some appeal over the long haul. Once that choice is made, the self-branding project we are talking about here can be aggressively pursued.

Building your own brand doesn't necessarily free you from corporate America. It takes smarts to know when to promote your own interests and when to promote your employer's. And you have to be careful what you become known for. Brands can box you in, so choose your expertise wisely.

One thing's for sure: it's better to brand yourself than to spend all your time branding a company that will escort you to the door with a cardboard box as soon as "things change."

"In most business settings, 'manager' is a special role set aside for the biggest sucker, the one who is willing to do the owner's dirty work in exchange for a chance to boss people around. I've been that sucker many times."

Chase Skills, Not Dollars (and Management Is for Suckers)

It's hard to master life without mastering business, and it's hard to master business when you're slogging it out on the lower rungs of the service industry. Some people are truly stuck, but others have a nasty habit of taking dead-end jobs because "the money is too good to pass up." Later, they hit a bitter ceiling.

I didn't know diddly-squat after I graduated from college. Looking back at all the ill-advised decisions I made, I did have one redeeming impulse: I craved new skills, and I was willing to suffer financially to get them. At one point, I took a job for forty dollars a week editing a new publication. That's one way to break into a field.

When you're willing to work for pennies, doors open. At the time I took my editorial "job," friends waiting tables were banking way more than I was. But I had this fanciful notion that my real compensation was the business education I was receiving. It might be the only thing from that entire era I was right about.

Often times, jobs that have the most cash incentives – bartending, waiting tables, and entry-level sales positions – don't have a big skills upside. (Though true sales jobs, where you prospect and close leads, are *vastly superior* to retail "sales" environments where your biggest responsibility is getting sweaters to scan properly.)

"Management" positions can be even more dangerous. In most business settings, manager is a special role set aside for the biggest sucker, the one who is willing to do the owner's dirty work in exchange for a chance to boss people around. I've been that sucker many times. The difference in compensation is usually a lot less than the "take one for the team" sacrifices expected. Management experience is valuable to a point, but as a general rule, it's better to have a life than to get stuck acting like an owner but being paid like an employee.

Skeptics of this line of thinking might find this example telling. An ice cream store near my office recently held a contest to guess the number of jelly beans in a jar. The sign they posted announced the winner's name, and proudly stated: "So how do we know there were 1,860 beans in the jar? Because our store manager counted each one of them."

Full disclosure: I currently manage people for my biggest client. It all depends on what you're getting out of it. In this case, my situation doesn't feel stagnant, and I have a profit-sharing agreement in place. But I've been in crummy management situations before, the kind where you work way too hard for an extra quarter an hour and a bigger set of keys. You can get lost in management "careers." The trick is to learn just enough about management to acquire the skills you need to push your own ventures forward. Either that, or acquire some real equity in the company you are toiling for.

The preferred approach to job selection is simple: "chase the skills, and the money will follow." There are no absolute rules – all you need is a knack for knowing when a job is drying up. If you head towards the biggest challenge, and switch jobs ruthlessly to find those challenges, taking promotions when they have a skills upside, you're on the right track. Notice that this approach clashes with how hiring managers want us to play.

Try dropping this line during an interview: "I'm here to learn as much as I can from your company, but as soon as I've outgrown this situation, I'll be moving on." You've just broken a cardinal rule by stating your self-interest; no offer will be forthcoming. Never mind that your future employer would do the same to you in a heartbeat.

Think of your business know-how as a container, and your cash flow as the water. Most people have pretty leaky containers. It doesn't matter how much cash you throw into a leaky container; it all streams out the bottom. So what makes for a strong container? Some think it's about tracking every expense and clipping coupons. At best, that's just the beginning.

It's not as simple as treating expenses like Whack-A-Mole, popping each in the head whenever it pokes up. All expenses are not created equal; sometimes you have to spend money to make more of it. So we have to understand the power of investing, and that means grasping financial documents like balance sheets and profit and loss statements. Strengthening our grip on cash flow requires more than just financial intelligence; it also involves marketing, sales and project management skills. You can learn some of this on your own, but the best place to pick it up is on the job.

By learning how a business invests, earns, and spends, you can apply that to your own situation. (We'll get into the nitty gritty of how to do that soon.) Companies assess human resources both in terms of their current needs and their overall strategic direction. We should adopt this same approach, continually assessing the tradeoffs of our work and heading towards the skills we need the most. When we get seriously off track, it's time for a career change.

For some, this smacks of disloyalty. It's not easy to put our own interests first. We are conditioned to give everything to our employers, and they are more than willing to take it. But if you are stagnating, you won't perform at your highest level. By pursuing the best work situations, you bring out the best in yourself. And that's the real meaning of loyalty.

"Experts are at the beck and call of their expertise. It is wonderful to feel indispensable – until that terrifying day when you realize you are chained to your desk."

Moving Beyond the Cult of the Expert

To free yourself from corporate America, you need to join the cult of the expert, and then renounce it. The second part takes a bit more doing.

The logic of becoming an expert is easy to understand: to compete against big companies, you need to excel at something that has been overlooked by mass marketers. The way to develop that niche is by becoming an expert at something.

In an earlier chapter, we talked about the distinction between an expert and "aficionado." The way I am using the term, "expert" implies that you have mastered a talent that has (or will soon have) a market value. Aficionado (as I am using it) means you have mastered something entertaining but financially useless.

Aficionado means you are good at something, but the world is indifferent. Harry Potter figurine collections, hair band memorabilia shrines, and fantasy football leagues are examples of aficionado activities. Indulge them by all means – as long as you have cash to burn or are comfortable treading water financially. At certain points in life, it's fine to coast.

Those of us with bills to pay and ambitions to satisfy need to take our heads out of the crossword puzzle and develop a meaningful expertise. How do you know when you've become a marketable expert? That's an easy one. You'll know because the phone will ring, and it won't be a telemarketer. You'll be approached with new job offers, new business partnerships, and speaking opportunities.

That's the point where most people screw up. They start to buy into their own hype, becoming infatuated with how billable they are. It's true that being a sought-after expert is a big step. It means you have options. No matter what kind of messed-up job you wind up in, your niche is a better parachute than any kind of severance package. But unless you can gross millions yelling at companies like ESPN's Dick Vitale does, the cult of the expert is a trap.

It's a trap because you can't step away. If you're not billable, you're not making money. And the more sophisticated your expertise is, the harder it is to train someone to step in when life throws you a curve ball or an extreme sports accident.

Expertise tends to tie you down, which is why this book's focus is a bit different. Our aim is to accumulate the resources to reclaim the ultimate commodity: our own time, spent as we see fit. Work when you want, on your own terms. Experts generally can't do that. Experts are at the beck and call of their expertise. Yeah, it's wonderful to feel indispensable – until that terrifying day when you realize you are chained to your desk.

The happiest entrepreneurs I know built systems on top of their expertise – systems that were easily taught to others. Once you figure out how to stay billable, take it one step further and remove yourself from the equation. You do that by creating teachable processes and cash flow streams that other people can manage. You want to create "turnkey" operations – businesses that run out of the box, businesses that smart high school students could run.

The harder it is to teach someone what you do, the further away you are. I am still too far away. I lean on my expertise in the SAP marketplace to foot my bills. My eventual goal is to create assets that others can manage. Publishing is one route to that goal. True, I'm the only one who can write the books (unless I commission other authors), but I can definitely teach people to handle the other aspects of publishing (especially marketing and publicity) that take up so much time. I've found that I can sell ten times more books without ten times the effort.

I used to thrive on feeling indispensable; now I see it as a warning sign that I'm headed in the wrong direction again. At this point in my career, there's nothing worse than a list of tasks on my plate that only I can do. It's on me to come up with business models that are easily implemented by others. The real riddle is to find a way to do what you love without letting it grind you. True, at the highest billable level, you can afford to be a solo-flying expert because you're banking so much per hour (entertainment lawyer, game show host, talking head). But the rest of us are better off cultivating systems.

Real-life examples of teachable systems span across industries. I've seen people do it with staffing firms, database consulting, and even restaurants. I wouldn't wish the restaurant business on my worst enemy, but the most successful restaurant owners *are* able to turn their operations over to managers – if they have their egos under enough control to step away. You can't free yourself until you get over yourself.

There's nothing wrong with being an expert at something. It's certainly a lot better than being a generic middle manager whom companies can hire and fire at will. But unless our goal is to work ourselves into the ground, expertise is ultimately a trap – unless our expertise is training other people to run our businesses.

Of course, even if you realize that you are stuck in the "expert trap," it's not always easy to break free from it. One step towards breaking free from being tied to billable hours is to build a real "marketing platform" that allows you to connect to your audience on a broader scale.

A "platform" gives you the ability to market products and services and generate passive income streams that are not tied to being a billable expert. I'll cover this in more detail in my "Internet Changes Everything" chapter, but for now, I would suggest that anyone who is dazzled by the appeal of being a sought-after expert should begin the less glamorous process of building a marketing platform instead.

Most of us are scrambling to get by, so we have a hard time imagining the downside to getting paid to babble on about things we are good at. And it's true that a marketable expertise can really expand your career options.

But there will come a time when the only thing you want is the one thing you can't "expert" your way out of: to step away from the wheel without having the bus run off the road. There is nothing more frustrating than knowing your ventures cannot do without you for more than a couple of days. And on the flip side, there is nothing more satisfying than income earned with little ongoing effort. To me, that is the true definition of "passive income," and the more passive your income is, the freer your life can be.

But developing truly passive income is no easy trick. Most of our so-called assets dry up as soon as we step away. The solution? A combination of perseverance and a willingness to question what success really means and how to get there. Profit should be measured at least partially by how much life energy we expend to get it.

I have referred to my friend who makes a bunch of money through his Web site traffic. Between advertising revenue and book sales, he is doing well, and his ongoing workload is minimal. Some months I make more money than he does, but by the standard of time-versus-money, he is *by far* the more successful businessperson. So join the cult of the expert, but move beyond it as soon as you possibly can.

"As we hit the open market, we are subjected to a necessary and painful feedback loop that shows us which ideas others will pay for and which they could care less about."

Gut Check #3: From the Lab to the Marketplace

So we've got a better handle on how to position ourselves while we're slogging it out for our current employer. Meanwhile, we've also been down in the lab developing our own assets. It's now time to take those assets to the marketplace.

This next phase is where the artists amongst us tend to falter. Most of us are a lot more comfortable doing our thing than selling ourselves. Successful ventures require both. Assets without a market are not going to generate income. Sometimes you have to create the market, other times you have to figure out how to enter an existing marketplace.

Each venture has it own marketing strategy. Sometimes it makes sense to sell ourselves; other times it's better to engage an agent or broker. As we hit the open market, we are subjected to a necessary and painful "feedback loop" that shows us which of our ideas others will pay for and which they could care less about. The lessons are not easy ones, but as we'll discuss, we can use the Internet to accelerate that feedback loop without emptying our wallets.

In the following chapters, we'll cover the areas of sales, marketing, and deal-making that we need to master if we want to produce income instead of spinning wheels. We'll look at why we are all salespeople whether we like it or not, and we'll see how most money is made or lost in a handful of deal-making moments we need to be ready for. For those who are looking ahead, after these topics are tackled, we'll move on to the issue of financial competency, and then we'll be on the home stretch.

In the upcoming section, I'll make sure to cover some of the popular approaches towards launching businesses, such as franchising, multi-level marketing, and venture capital. As you might expect, I view those options with more than a bit of skepticism.

Part VI:

Taking Your Assets to Market

We Are All Salespeople

The Rules of the Deal (and the Freedom to Walk Away)

The Internet Changes Everything (Or Maybe Not)

Outsource Everything – How to Manage the Cash/Time Crossover

Protecting Your Advantage – How to Create Barriers to Entry

Making Fun of Business Plans, Venture Capital, and Multi-Level Marketing

Gut Check #4: Making the Money We Earn Count

"You don't have to look conventional to succeed – but you do have to master the rules of the game in order to break them. And you can't learn the game folding shirts at The Gap."

We Are All Salespeople

I'm going to lose some sensitive artists, but it has to be said: we are all selling something. Those who view salespeople with contempt are still selling something: contempt for salespeople. Of course, what they are really selling is the image of someone with too much rebel integrity for the world of commerce.

Usually someone else is financing their rebellion. At my college, we had the phenomenon of the trust fund hippie. The students who looked the most like homeless people were the ones with the biggest credit lines.

You can't become a rebel icon without brilliant sales and marketing. Kurt Cobain reeked of indifference to commerce. You couldn't pick him out of a lineup of Seattle panhandlers. But he was only able to capitalize on that image because he had a sales and marketing engine behind him.

When you have genius-level talent, you can have a Trent Reznor/Kurt Cobain scorn for commerce while your handlers don the suits and ties. Geniuses get to act eccentric and leave the chores of moving product to their representatives.

But unless you're a genius with good market timing, contempt for sales and marketing is not just going to make you a hypocrite – it's also going to make you broke. The coolest-looking people in my town have the worst jobs. These are the tattooed hipsters with tongue piercings and wallet chains. Later you find them slouched behind a counter selling you pre-ripped jeans.

Dressing cool is one thing – figuring out how to work the system on your own terms is a whole other animal. You don't have to look conventional to succeed – but you do have to master the rules of the game in order to break them. And you can't learn the game folding shirts at The Gap or selling vintage gear at a store you don't own, where the only perk is being able to wear torn fishnets.

You may be wondering how this rant fits into the flow of the book. Once we develop our assets, we have to deal with the marketplace, and the market has no patience for our desire to be cool. We still have to work a room. Unless we know something about sales and marketing, we'll be stuck with "assets" that are either worthless or might as well be, since we have no ability to turn them into cash flow.

The power of sales and marketing is the abiding lesson of Apple versus Microsoft. It's the cautionary tale of a vastly inferior product (early PCs) beating a vastly superior product (early Macs). The difference was marketing. Apple was happy with high profitability in niche markets. Microsoft relentlessly marketed a poor product and sold a ton.

Microsoft then used the cash from its early success to drastically improve their product while rendering Apple a niche player. Microsoft also redefined the market from a personal computer market to an operating systems market. Initially, Apple didn't want to make money on computers it didn't make. Microsoft focused its marketing and product development on software and let other companies build machines. Of course, Apple has made some brilliant moves in recent years, proving they have learned the importance of well-executed marketing, but Apple has never threatened the dominance of the Windows operating system. Microsoft now faces new open source threats, but none of them were Apple's doing.

Unfortunately, most of us (including myself) are more like Apple. We want to live in a world where quality will eventually triumph. If we create something beautiful, goes this wishful line of thinking, our audience will come. But there's more great writing in journals and attic chests than you'll ever find in a magazine rack. Publishing requires much more than an act of creation. Most successful writers I know are actually mediocre talent-wise. They *do* have two qualities: perseverance and a knack for making connections. And most of them have a specialty market of readers they understand. Creative talent is a nice-to-have and that's it.

We want to climb by the merits of our work, but sadly, you can more accurately equate people's success not by their inherent talent, but by their ability to sell themselves. I've never met a skilled marketer or salesperson who struggled to make money. That doesn't mean I always like how salespeople come across, but I've gained respect for how they always seem to land on their feet.

It's rare to run into companies with great marketing and sales teams that are going under financially. If your marketing people are brilliant and your salespeople can sell, business slowdowns are simply an opportunity to reposition your services and give your sales team something else to sell.

Most of the business failures I've seen over the years were tied to weak sales or marketing. This is especially true for smaller companies, where owners get busy running the business and forget about marketing and sales strategy. If you're not building that sales pipeline, you're headed for a dry season sooner or later.

There are two reasons why people shun sales. One is because they don't want to participate in the ugly business of selling in order to succeed. The other is because they don't believe they can sell. "I'm not a salesperson," they will tell you, as they write their own pink slips.

I'm not denying the phenomenon of the born salesperson. You know the type: they launched their first lemonade stand when they were six years old; later they sold pizza out of their dorm room. A born salesperson can sell anything to anybody. I got a punishing lesson in this type of personality when I tried to sell season theater tickets to cash-strapped residents of Tulsa, Oklahoma, in the summer of '86.

I worked the job a month and didn't sell a single ticket. The workplace was one big table with a bunch of phones around it. My mediocrity was on public display. One woman at the table was able to sell ten season tickets or more a night. Customers seemed to give her the sale just to get her off the phone.

We look at people like that and think, "I could never do that, so I'm not a salesperson." Then we shut the door on improving those skills. It's true that only a minority of people can sell anything to anybody. The rest of us can also be effective, but here's the catch: we have to sell something we believe in. Successful salespeople have a range of personalities. Some have the gift of gab; others feel a pit in their stomach when they make a cold call. Styles vary; a passion for what they sell is the constant.

We cannot take our assets to market without sales abilities. We don't necessarily have to sell our own work, but we do need to know enough about sales to manage those who represent us. I have friends who count on their agents to represent them. But before an agent took them on, they too had to be sold.

I am not the world's best salesperson. But I've gotten to the point where I can call anybody. I've also gotten better at marketing myself. Few people buy a product until they encounter it numerous times. The more you are able to make people aware of your product (branding), put them in a position to buy, and then close them on the deal, the better things will go for you. And this goes for activists as well as businesspeople.

It's not selling that makes you corrupt; it's what you sell that defines you. Who's a bigger sellout – the band that sells its songs online in as many places as possible, or the band that refuses to "sell out" and therefore plays in obscurity while working jobs they can't stand? Sometimes the only way to avoid selling out is to learn how to sell something. As for those who think genius gives them a pass, I would reconsider.

I'm not going to argue that Journey are musical geniuses, but if they came along now, they'd learn a hard lesson about timing. So would Frank Zappa, and he actually was a genius. But geniuses without markets are no more immune to poverty and obscurity than we are. Skillful marketing helps you change timing by changing the playing field. You do this by altering the perception in people's minds about what they need. No one is knocking on my door asking for this book, but if I market it well enough, I hope to create a demand for it.

Just remember that marketing assets is every bit as difficult as developing them. To be truly successful, you need skills on both sides. This is the long-denied unity between the creative process (creating assets) and the business side (marketing and selling those assets). If you believe in the value of the assets you've created, you should have no qualms about selling them to as many people as possible. Money actually comes in handy. Make enough money and you can even buy your way into a presidential debate.

If that's not enough to convince you that sales matters, I'll close by saying that aside from musicians, the people I've known who are most successful at finding relationships are all salespeople. Salespeople are just comfortable with the numbers game. They are used to being turned down and don't get hung up on it. If you don't think that's a useful skill, you probably haven't been single in a while.

"Negotiation gurus will tell you that there is always a win-win outcome you should pursue. Others advise you to see the person across the table as an adversary. Throw out that formulaic junk."

The Rules of the Deal (and the Freedom to Walk Away)

If you can't cut a deal, you won't succeed. You make most of your money when you finalize a contract. Whether you're negotiating a land purchase or an employment offer, the money is made when the deal is done. When you leave money on the table, you're *not* getting it back later.

We've all accepted job offers with low base salaries because we were duped by the usual bogus assurances: "We'll bump up your salary in six months," or "We'll cover the rest in bonuses." Getting it in writing doesn't help. There are a million ways to sleaze out of a contract, and your employer's legal team is a tad better financed than yours.

Get the money on the front end. There are loads of books on negotiation, so I'm not going to waste unnecessary time on it here, except to say this: people are tied to corporate America because they can't cut a better deal for themselves. Cutting a better deal comes down to two things that can be taught (strategy and leverage), and one thing that can't (guts).

The strategy of the deal is not as complicated as the negotiation wonks would have you believe. The most important negotiation tool is leverage. Leverage is just a buzz word (I call them "wank words") that translates into common sense as "you are only as powerful as your options." The more options you have, the stronger your position. There is an art to realizing when you have leverage and when you don't – the terrain is constantly shifting.

To get the best possible deal, you have to be able to walk away. Having options allows you to win the best possible terms. The kicker is that most of the time, both parties in a deal are mutually dependent and cannot walk away without a price. That's where strategy comes in – knowing how to get the most you can based on the leverage you have.

Some would argue you can accomplish this by bluffing. That's true, but it requires real gamesmanship. Bluffing is a tactic better saved for penny ante card games. In negotiation, you gamble only if the cost of losing is one you (and your family) can live with. I have a less conventional take on negotiation: I believe you get the most by playing the hand you've been dealt as well as you can and not playing games.

Some negotiation gurus will tell you that there is always a "win-win" outcome you should pursue. Others advise you to see the persons across the table as an adversary looking out for their own best interest at the expense of your own. Following the adversarial way of negotiating, you should always bid higher than what you are willing to settle for, with the assumption being that the other person has a number in mind somewhere in the middle. They'll wait for you to come down and meet them halfway.

Throw out that formulaic junk. The only rule of negotiation is that each situation is different. Sometimes there is a win-win outcome; sometimes there is only one prize and no fair way to divide it. Sometimes it's better to give a little more than you planned, even when your leverage is strong, in the interests of future business.

Lording your (often temporary) advantage over a business partner can backfire. And don't forget that negotiations generally involve more than one point of agreement. In a salary negotiation, for example, you might bend on total salary and concentrate your focus on scoring extra vacation time.

In any deal, there are usually several talking points. Sometimes you "win" a deal by approaching it creatively, conceding the point the other party cares about most and then proposing (and winning) another point that's more important to you. Of course, the stronger the hand you bring to the table, the fewer the concessions you will have to bend on.

Returning to this book's themes, if the key to winning negotiations is having options, it's time to develop those options. Sometimes you have to settle for a bad deal, start from scratch, and try to improve your position in life. Once you develop marketable, cash-generating assets, you'll find that negotiating is a lot easier.

But you don't have to wait to put these tactics to work. Whenever we have a valuable skill, we can use these techniques to achieve a market value for that skill. There are times when we are a hot commodity – perhaps we have a technical skill that is in demand, or we find ourselves in an industry that is taking off. That's when we need to make our move and get the best job offer we can.

Boosting revenues is a key to getting off the corporate treadmill. Down the road, it is preferable that we have more revenue sources than wages, since wages are taxed more heavily than investment income. But a more aggressive salary is a good start. We can also use negotiating tactics to get the job skills we need. Skills pave the way.

Behind a winning deal is basic trust in our gut instincts. I went through a decade of business mistakes before I finally started trusting what my gut was telling me all along. Up to that point, I thought there was something mysterious about business. I didn't go with my instincts because I figured that I was too inexperienced. End result: I ended up in bed with the wrong people.

You know in your gut when you're dealing with sketchy individuals and too-good-to-be-true proposals. But when you don't have a lot of experience, the tendency is to go along. Never go along. Business, in the end, is mostly about relationships. Sometimes these relationships are enabled by technology, but it's still people dealing with people. The good sense you learned navigating the streets and the playground is exactly what you need in a "sophisticated" business context.

Success in business is simply combining relationships with some kind of industry-specific ability or trade that gives you an edge. Combine that with deal-making skills and you're well on your way. I emphasize negotiation for two reasons: one, you need those skills to get the best salary, and two, you need them even more when you launch your own ventures. I've seen so many businesses fail because people set up shop with the wrong partners or sold off too much control to investors. How we negotiate the ownership of a venture has a lot to do with its ultimate success.

My favorite deal-making strategy of all: mix bread-and-butter "keep the lights on" deals with speculative, high-incentive deals. When there is no cash coming in, you have to stay practical: get a bread-and-butter deal (or job) that will keep the bills paid. But once that's in place, you are now in the position to take a chance. So the next deal might be one with high upside.

Since you can afford to take no money upfront on the high upside deal, you can structure it in terms of incentives. In the world of deal-making, the less cash you need as a down payment, the more you can get in the payout. This makes sense – by taking less cash, you are minimizing the risk for your partner.

Your profits will be greater if things work out, but your partner can live with that because you are contributing your "sweat" for nothing.

So close a cash-first deal to keep creditors at bay, but after that, roll the dice. This way, you can strike high upside deals without having to bluff or expose yourself. There are many ways you can structure deals to take advantage of this incentive-based philosophy. You saw a lot of this in the dotcom era.

I worked with several technical firms that built Web sites in exchange for stock options. They took enough cash upfront to keep the lights on; the rest they took in stock options. You can still do deals this way, though not every company is willing to give up equity for services. You can also use this approach as a salesperson, starting with a high base salary but moving to pure commission once the cash starts flowing.

When I started my own business in the summer of 2000, I had enough money from real estate that I was able to strike a high incentive deal with a technology staffing firm. We built their Web site at no charge in exchange for a percentage of all job placements made from the resumes that came in.

On paper, it was a fantastic deal, but market circumstances changed. We still made close to $50,000 from deals off that site – far better compensation than we would have gotten if we had done a traditional fee-for-services Web design arrangement. Compared to our total time investment, that deal was not a huge success, but it was worth the dice roll.

Those with something to fall back on are not only able to take on high incentive deals, they are also much better equipped to handle the setbacks of employed-at-will. I know a salesperson who was fired recently. I called him an hour after it happened and he actually sounded happy. Ever since his early 20s, he has been putting his commission checks into real estate. It's a lot easier to handle pink slips when you own ten rental properties.

I have another colleague who bills out on technical projects at $150 an hour. She works hard to keep her skills current and it pays off. She is one of those rare businesspeople who speaks her mind (even in front of her clients) without fearing the consequences. People sense that she is in demand and therefore free to walk away, and they treat her with more respect as a result.

The stronger your financial position gets, the more leverage on corporate America you have. At some point, you don't have to work at all (or for six months, or a year, etc.). The greatest power in the world is the power to walk away.

From that point on, you can negotiate terms that will not only get your side ventures rolling, but make your career more enjoyable, and yes, more lucrative. There's more to life than getting paid. But there are few things sweeter than getting paid what you're worth.

"A well-designed Web site makes a ragtag team look legit. I've ordered products from people who probably had pretty lousy hygiene."

The Internet Changes Everything – Or Maybe Not

Remember all the idiots who said that the Internet was going to change everything? I was one of them. Yep, I was a card-carrying member of the mid-90s gold rush. The money felt queasy, but I still wanted a piece. The Internet's value to businesses has swung back and forth ever since. Where we're at now: a pretty good market for smaller players with attitude like you and me.

True, giants like Amazon are now entrenched, but the Internet still provides an avenue for those who want to test new businesses without risking more than they can afford to lose. And it's a great place to experiment with the feedback loop – you can get near-instant response on new products. You can also get a good handle on the popularity of your pages by crunching traffic stats until your eyes dry out.

Ever since the mid-90s, companies have been trying to figure out how to (wank word warning) "monetize" their Web sites. The obstacles have changed, but the challenge continues. As of this writing, YouTube is getting a lot of business press for how much money it is losing despite the site's huge popularity.

There was a point in the late 90s where advertising was supposed to save struggling Web site sites and solve their revenue problems. But the first wave of Internet advertising collapsed. Banner ad rates came down to earth as companies wised up to the fact that intrusive, one-size-fits-all advertising has severe limitations.

In the last couple years, Internet advertising has made a comeback thanks to the Google "contextual ad" phenomenon. Google Adwords is now just one form of embedded advertising that is driven by keywords. You can see these ads on the right side of Google's search listings. But more importantly, you now see Google-type ads on all kinds of Web sites. Any Web site with a decent amount of traffic can now use this type of advertising as a revenue stream.

Enterprising folks such as AskDaveTaylor.com can make a pretty good living solely through hosting these ads on their sites. "AskDave" goes extreme, forcing you to smack into those Google ads early and often, but you can opt for a subtler approach than AskDave and still make money. You might not be able to live on Google ads alone, but they can certainly be a leg on your revenue table. Even if Google doesn't come through for you, other firms that relate to your industry might want to pay to be seen on your site.

It's simply a matter of creating appealing content and services around your niche focus. In many cases, a good chunk of that content can be user-created – if you build a platform that users like. Once you do that, you can get the traffic. And once you get the traffic, you can usually get the ads (or consulting leads). And these days, with a savvy design, you can even get your users to build out some of the content for you. The Flickr.com sensation is one such example.

Contextual ads make a big difference in the Internet economy: you don't have to be ESPN.com to attract an advertiser's attention. The days of "if you build it, they will come" have returned – though without the evangelical zeal this time around.

You can see this even in the case of YouTube, which built a hugely popular site without a business model and then sold it to Google before I could finish this chapter.

Build a site, get traffic, put ads/relevant products on site, make money. Involve your users early and often. Ad revenues are crucial because consumers won't pay for much content on a subscription basis besides porn. There are exceptions: ESPN has found a way to charge users a modest amount per year to access their Insider program, but even CNN.com, which tried charging for its video content, had to revert back to offering video for free, using an advertising-based model instead.

Knowing that this approach works sets us free: we can now build sites that cater to our interests. Keep in mind: not all consumer groups are created equal in the eyes of advertisers, but just about any site that has significant traffic can convert some of that traffic into ad revenue. Of course, the most effective sites have multiple revenue streams, combining advertising with paid premium services and mail order products.

A small publisher, for example, would have advertising as well as an online bookstore where customers can order books. Informative free content and book samples would drive people to the site and provide fodder for search engines. Site visitors might be given the option to write their own book reviews or rate the content they see.

Of course, some folks have enough industry connections to build Web sites that target businesses instead of consumers (this is typically called "B2B" as opposed to "B2C"). If you can attract businesses to your site, you may be able to charge more than you could with a consumer-driven site.

But the Internet is more than a revenue stream. For many businesses, the real value of the Internet is relationship-building and product education. Customers now routinely research products online before they buy. You can get a real feel for a company's offerings through a well-developed Web site. And of course a company can develop a nice database of prospects by compiling email lists from folks who sign up to receive product updates or free content.

Once you develop enough Web traffic, your site will be indexed by search engines frequently enough that you will be able to identify visitor trends in a matter of days or even hours. And search engines, particularly Google's, are biased towards sites that offer quality content.

Scoring a prominent place in search engine results can drive prospects to a business and save a huge amount of money on marketing. Even conventional brick-and-mortar ventures, such as restaurants, can benefit from a well-thought Web site that attracts new customers, offers halfway accurate driving directions, and builds its brand via local and national "portals" that tourists scour.

No, the Internet can't eliminate business risk. There still comes a time when you have to take the leap and go "all in." But the Internet makes it much more affordable to roll out new business ideas without the empty-your-wallet marketing required by a traditional business startup. And the Internet makes it *much* easier to take advantage of the "feedback loop."

Most of the email you get from your site will probably be annoying, but all of it (barring herbal Viagra spam) will be invaluable. By posting this book online as I wrote it, I put a lot of reader feedback to use. I don't know how good you think the final book is, but it's much better because of those who took the time to point out its flaws online.

One of the best things about using the Internet for a launching point: once you have significant traffic, you can adjust your business model to the needs of that audience. You can think of a popular Web site as a marketing test zone where a variety of services and products can be offered until something sticks.

And you can do this across industries, adjusting your tone and pitch to the demographics of your visitors.

One big disclaimer: you have to be honest about which of your projects are in demand and which are not. Sometimes what people are interested in comes as a big surprise. One of the reasons I built a new SAP career site is because I get plastered with emails from SAP consultants asking me for advice.

You ignore that level of demand at your own peril. The trick is to turn the popular topics into revenue streams so that you can finance other dreamier projects without having to worry about how people will receive them.

People make too much of slaying giants on the Internet. You're not going to beat Amazon or eBay at the online game. But even Facebook is a fairly recent invention, so there's still room for bad ideas to go big. The best thing: a well-designed Web site makes a ragtag team look legit. I've ordered products from people who probably had pretty lousy hygiene, but I've never been burned. (Well, there's one punk in New Jersey who trashed me on eBay.)

So if advertising can play such an important part in a small enterprise, why aren't there ads on FreeFromCorporateAmerica.com? Fair question. In business terms, it's a mistake not to put ads on that site. I don't have a good reason, except that it feels wrong. I feel the same way about JonReed.net. There are times when ads can cheapen a venture, or imply that your motivations are about getting paid first and everything else second. Sometimes that's true, but sometimes it's not.

Example: I recently launched a new SAP Web site for my SAP podcasts and market analysis (JonERP.com), and I've already developed enough traffic to make about $500 a month in advertising and lead sharing of various kinds. It might seem odd that I would take ad money on one site and not another. I just want to make sure with FreeFromCorporateAmerica.com that people see these ideas are not compromised by corporate sponsors. But I know that advertising will be crucial to some of my other ventures.

Despite its quirky ups and downs, the Internet can help us, but it will never again substitute for business acumen. It's just a tool we can use to launch ventures on the cheap and accelerate the feedback loop. The time we spend mastering the Internet might not help us win the "cool competition," but we'll have the satisfaction of knowing how to test business ideas, and maybe find the one that can change our lives for the better.

It's important to keep in mind that you can use the Internet to your advantage even if you have no intention of starting a business. You can also use the Internet to build that mystical thing referred to in the publishing industry as a "platform." Your platform is how you connect to your audience or industry.

Whether or not you are an aspiring author, the best way to start the transition from being a billable expert to being someone with passive income streams is to build a marketing platform. A platform is something that not every well known "expert" has.

For example, if your company did all your branding for you, then you don't have your own Web site or email list. If you leave that company, you have to build your platform from scratch – though you do have some name recognition to help you. The bigger your online audience for what you do, the bigger a "platform" you can have. A direct "snail mail" list is part of a platform also, but the Internet is uniquely well suited for building a marketing engine. And once you have built it, you are in a much better position to call your own shots and develop additional revenue streams. For example, you could use such a "platform" to generate consulting leads to take on in addition to your current work, and perhaps begin the transition towards hiring other people and putting systems into place.

No, the Internet is not going to change everything. Anyone who ever said that in the past, including myself, feels kind of silly now. But when it comes to good business, becoming a bit of an Internet geek is not such a bad idea after all.

"People congratulate themselves because they do their own taxes and change their own oil. That's great – if they want to become accountants or mechanics."

Outsource Whatever You Can – How to Master the Cash/Time Crossover

Being a businessperson isn't that great. Getting paid is cool, but poring over Excel formulas and PowerPoints isn't. To make business seem a little more hip-hop, companies make up buzzwords so that the work they do sounds sexy and important. One such buzzword is "core competency." The phrase is may be a little yesterday, but the message is definitely today.

I like to make fun of buzzwords – I even did my own version of "Wank Words Bingo" so that people could holler "bingo" when someone said "white board" one too many times in a meeting. Bingo aside, most corporate buzzwords conceal an important concept we should make use of.

That is true of core competency, which essentially means "focus on what you are good at." You might be thinking, "That's just common sense," and you'd be right. But here's where it gets interesting: it's not that easy to focus on one thing. You can't barter fish for shoes anymore. In your new venture, if you don't want to do something yourself, you have to pay someone to do it. And your profit margin can't always spare the difference. Thus the late-night bookkeeper.

So we can pat ourselves on the back and talk core competencies, but only the most successful businesses are able to free up their people to do the one thing they are best at. Focusing on what we do best is a luxury most can't afford, but it's still what we should shoot for. Do what you excel at – outsource everything else. And by "outsourcing," we don't necessarily mean sending work offshore – we simply mean finding someone else to take the distracting stuff off our plates.

In the corporate world, outsourcing has taken on a negative connotation, implying the utilization of the global labor pool to cut costs. Sometimes this is referred to as "offshoring." The ethics of these practices are subject to debate, but there's no question that the strategic use of outsourcing is utilized by companies who are catering to cost-conscious consumers on the one hand, and expectant shareholders on the other. You see this in the Information Technology marketplace, where programming work is sourced to a variety of overseas locations. According to Eric Keller in his book *Technology Paradise Lost*, Information Technology outsourcing, properly managed, can save up to 70 percent of programming costs.

The corporate tactic of outsourcing has relevance because we can employ it without facing the dilemma of sending jobs overseas. For us, outsourcing simply means doing what we do best and hiring others to do the rest. We can hire them from anywhere. More likely than not, we'll hire the neighbor who does a little Web design on the side.

The growth of our side ventures softens the blows of pink slip culture. There's nothing more satisfying than putting money in friends' pockets – especially for work we created from our own imagination and business model.

Corporate America is suffering from outsourcing creep. The offshoring of technical work is gradually spreading to other white collar information worker jobs. Overseas call centers are one such example. Even if you have no plans to start a side venture, the realities of global labor can (and should) impact your own career planning.

Another book to consider is Daniel Pink's *A Whole New Mind.* In Pink's book, he explains how to transform our skills from left brain/information-driven to right brain/creative, thereby making ourselves more "outsourcing proof." But Pink doesn't go far enough. Changing your skill set is not enough to ensure financial security, because career security and financial security are no longer the same thing. Thus the need for side ventures and assets we control.

When we get our ventures off the ground, we typically do most of the work ourselves. But if (and when) money starts flowing, we will hit some cash/time crossover points. Cash/time crossover is simply the point where it is no longer efficient for us to do a particular task ourselves.

There are a number of things you could outsource. Two of the most common are bookkeeping and (usually a bit later on) payroll. There are way too many weekend bookkeepers. If you choose the right accountant, you can actually save money through timely advice. Other services, like third-party payroll, do not necessarily save money, but certainly save headaches, and quite possibly tax exposure. Some of these services can save a marriage.

One of the big trends of the Internet age is turning competitors into partners. Often, the best way to focus on your core is to turn over secondary markets to a competitor in exchange for business leads or a percentage of business closed or whatever arrangement works out. This is the modern equivalent of "shoes for fish," and it can work, though it's not always easy. You really have to grit your teeth before handing off good business to competitors. But we have to pare down until we get to the core of what we excel at.

The less relevant the work is to that core, the more likely we should outsource it. That's why accounting and payroll are such good candidates. There are other times when it makes more sense to hire an employee. Hire internally when you need someone to help you with key business processes. That's the kind of knowledge you want to keep in-house. Otherwise, keep on outsourcing.

One thing people outsource too often (and pay way too much for) is marketing. Sometimes it's good to involve some outside marketing and publicity folks in your venture, but keep them at arm's length. We shouldn't even be in business if we don't understand enough about marketing to handle a campaign ourselves.

When we kicked off the publicity phase for *Resumes From Hell*, we got marketing bids in the tens of thousands of dollars. Those bids were full of the usual marketing fluff. Eventually, we found a firm that agreed to handle the occasional email campaign, but we wrote the content and owned the database after each mailing. This way, we kept costs down while taking advantage of outside talent.

This book is an extreme example of something you can't outsource because only I can write it. If I could hire monkeys to finish it, I would have done so already. Once my book is published, I will hire folks to help with the marketing phase. Until then, the work is on me. I have to be ruthless about stealing time. I also take advantage of the cash/time crossover by paying interns and office cleaners and anyone else I can sucker into my world.

The early stages of a venture are a great time to get exposure to all aspects of business. But eventually we need to hone in. We've got to be the best in the world at something, or in that ballpark, and that means consistency and focus. We can't do that when we're driving the payroll deposit to the bank on Fridays.

People congratulate themselves because they do their own taxes and change their own oil. That's great – if they want to become accountants or mechanics. Otherwise, they are better off with a specialization that plays to their strengths and builds on their core competencies. Did I hear someone yell bingo?

"I would go so far as to say that if you have no aspiring competition, there's a problem with your business model."

Protecting Your Advantage – How to Create Barriers to Entry

It's been a long time since I added a new chapter to this book. Since then, I put the book through a series of rewrites. I vowed not to expand it further. But one idea keeps coming up: barriers to entry. This concept is so important that I'm going to break my vow and sneak it into the book.

We've talked about becoming the best in the world at whatever it is you do. It's a key objective for anyone who wants to move freely in and out of corporate circles. When you are the best, or at least in the top tier, you can operate in the business world from a position of strength.

But here's the catch: you want to have some competition. If you're the only person in the world who is good at what you do, chances are there isn't much of a marketplace for your services. I joke about being one of the best in the world at writing about forgotten hair bands, but no one is knocking on my door about that. The best businesses attract competition because their market is attractive. I would go so far as to say that if you have no aspiring competition, there's a problem with your business model.

To a point, competition is a good thing – a sign that whatever you do has a quantifiable market. On the other hand, you don't want to make it easy for competitors to move in and do what you do. You want your specialty to be perceived as attractive, but to remain a little beyond the reach of those who want a piece of it. You do this by creating "barriers to entry." Corporate America is incredibly good at this. Large companies are well versed at locking smaller entities out through exclusive relationships no one else can breach.

One remote-tossing example is Direct TV's deal as the sole provider of the NFL Sunday Ticket. How many football fans have been forced to switch from cable to satellite because they had no access to games they wanted? This must drive the cable companies nuts – I know it drives me nuts – but all cable can do is lose football fans until the NFL's contract with Direct TV expires. Sure, Comcast can tell their customers that "we carry a bunch of obscure college football games every weekend," but for fans of the NFL, those games are an inferior product.

The level playing field is a myth. You've earned your market share. No way are you going to expose it to another business in search of green pastures. That's why it's better to master the rules of the game than to sit on the sidelines resenting the corporate entities that apply these rules to their advantage. To an extent, we can serve up the same medicine.

There are five barriers to entry we can take advantage of: innovation, exclusivity, patent, reputation, and location. Let's look at each of these in turn.

Innovation is the most subtle of the barriers to entry. Most companies are better at copying a good strategy than developing their own. That's why most people who stay ahead of the corporate game are natural innovators. Instead of resting on the revenues of their accomplishments, they are always tweaking and improving. Not because they are obsessive – well, maybe they are – but because they have a passion for what they do and a desire to excel. That means committing to a continuous state of improvement and re-invention. Innovation is a great tactic for those of us who are looking to free ourselves from corporate structures.

Corporations pay big lip service to innovation – just turn on a TV and you'll see plenty of commercials that trumpet corporate innovation, IBM's "building a smarter planet" series being one recent example – but the fact is that larger companies, by definition, move more slowly than smaller ones. Companies are not unlike ships. Yachts might be more comfortable, and they can certainly serve more passengers, but they can't change direction as fast as a little dinghy. Dinghies can get caught in the wake of a big ship, but if you stay ahead of the weather, it's not so bad being small and maneuverable.

Innovation is a valuable practice, but it's even more effective in conjunction with other tactics. We've already talked about exclusivity; there are few business tools more powerful than exclusive relationships. New businesses typically have trouble getting clients to agree to exclusive provider relationships, but as your business relationships deepen and you obtain a track record, asking for an exclusive relationship can be an important step.

Sometimes incentives are given to the other party in exchange for granting the exclusive; other times, the value of the exclusive is in knowing that they only have to turn to you for their needs, rather than wasting time fielding inquiries from other firms.

Exclusives can be applied to almost any field, and the definition of an exclusive can be expanded to include any form of creative control. For example, a small publishing company might sign a deal with an author that grants them exclusive rights or first options on any film rights or subsequent editions of the book title.

In the headhunting field, it is common to obtain an exclusive with a hiring manager for certain kinds of openings. This kind of relationship improves your chances of closing deals significantly. Whenever we are pursuing our business interests, we should be on the lookout for opportunities to deepen our business relationships through some sort of exclusive terms.

Patents are another excellent barrier to entry. (When we use the term "patents" here, we're talking about all forms of copyrighting and control over inventions and other creative products.) In some cases, control over these products falls automatically to the creator; but in others, you need to file the paperwork in order to claim that work yourself. I have known technical consultants who were able obtain ownership of work they performed as an employee that their employer was not interested in owning. Some of these folks are now doing very well selling their own product.

If you dig into the history of the big software companies, many of founders did the same thing, either purchasing the original software after developing it, or building it on the side and owning it from the beginning. Patents and copyrights are powerful because you don't necessarily have to build a business and marketing engine around them in order to benefit.

In some cases, such as a songwriter who has written a winning tune, you don't have any further work to do, except wait for the checks to come in each time your invention or creative work is used in a commercial context of some sort. And the best thing of all? Your competitors can't use or mimic your inventions without getting an intimidating letter from your lawyer.

Reputation is another barrier to entry. If you have a good reputation in a particular market, that means the repetition of your branding efforts has paid off – you now have an inherent name recognition advantage over competitors. Other companies might try to tap into your market, but you are the one your market knows and trusts.

In some fields, this trust factor can play a defining role in sales. Reputation has an impact in subtle ways also, including word-of-mouth referrals. Once I did some marketing for a band in search of a big record deal. I got the most interest from executives who had heard of them from previous albums and promotions. Reputation played a big role in the relative warmth of the cold calls.

The final barrier to entry is location. We can all appreciate the power of location, whether it's the mega-Wal-Mart sitting on top of a town we drive through on the way to work, or a restaurant that's nabbed the busiest corner of a major intersection. But we can expand the term "location" to apply to virtual locations as well, including preferred Web site URLs and how well a Web site ranks when relevant keywords are entered into search engines. Anytime you can get a corner on a popular location, you've simultaneously helped your chances and made it that much harder for someone else to copy you.

Let's look at how these concepts apply to my own market position. In the SAP field, I am known as the "SAP career expert." Others have tried to move into this turf over the years. To be fair, it's not the most coveted niche in the business world. But it has been a real asset to me in terms of professional opportunities and book sales. The fact that I have done this for upwards of ten years carries some weight. There is definitely name recognition there, which fits into reputation.

I have copyright/patent power in my first SAP book and the second one I am wrapping up now. I have exclusivity in my role as the career expert on one of the most frequented sites for SAP professionals. In terms of innovation, my new SAP Web site is a "Web 2.0" kind of site with career blog, podcasts, and even a Twitter feed. I have cornered some useful online locations also. I have mentioned that during the last two years, my

SAP consulting book has appeared in the top five results on Amazon when the term "SAP" is typed in.

So when you look at my market niche, all of the main barriers to entry come into play. It doesn't mean that other people can't make money in my areas of specialization – in fact, some do, and that is mostly a good thing, though I do have to keep a wary eye on the competition. In the SAP arena, making it tougher for others to duplicate what I do has definitely paid off. I doubt it is a coincidence that I have had more success in this area than in my other market niches where my barriers to entry are not nearly as comprehensive.

For some readers, the idea of constructing barriers to entry might seem like a hardcore tactic better suited for big businesses. But there is a ruthlessness to good business that cannot be denied. Big business tactics work for a reason. No, we don't have to endorse ugly monopolistic practices or use them to bludgeon our competition.

Some business practices may be legal, but they just feel wrong. We should all draw lines we can live with. The tactics I have described here are generally fair as long as they are fairly used. More often than not, we are the only ones looking out for our own interests. Knowing how to do that can make the difference between long-term prosperity and an all-too-brief glimpse.

"When I recall the giddiness former employers felt about their business plans, I feel a little seasick. Some of these plans sounded so good they should have been mounted and framed. But now they line gerbil cages."

Making Fun of Business Plans, Venture Capital, and Multi-Level Marketing

Readers have been after me. Through my Web site, I've been asked about classic entrepreneurial topics like business plans, venture capital, and multi-level marketing. I briefly dismissed business plans in an earlier chapter, but that raised more questions than answers. So let's go through each of these topics, as well as the tactic of franchising, in the context of this book's themes.

I have no major beef with business plans. I criticized them earlier because business is more about execution than salivating over the next big idea. I've read lots of business plans over the years; they all gushed with confidence. And yet, none of those companies exist today. Oh well, at least they looked successful on paper. When I recall the giddiness former employers felt about their "plans," I feel a little seasick (which is appropriate, since in some cases, I was indeed taken along for a ride). Some of these plans sounded so good they should have been mounted and framed. Now they line gerbil cages.

Sure, writing a business plan can be a great education. As you master the plan's components, such as marketing and financials, you learn how to tie those concepts into your business model. As a way to learn more about business, writing a business plan is a useful exercise. But the time you spend writing and researching can take you too far into theory. Some would call that an "opportunity cost." The real learning happens when you take those ideas and try to get customers to actually buy into them.

A particularly treacherous area of the business plan is the financials section. Most business plans crunch numbers until they come out right. You have to hold your nose from the stench of these over-inflated fantasy numbers. Fact: there's no way to pinpoint what the costs and revenues of a business are going to be. Contingencies are called contingencies for a reason.

Divorcing yourself from cool ideas that aren't financially viable takes ruthless honesty. Most people rework the numbers until their ideas look good, rather than reworking their ideas. The point of the exercise, of course, is to walk away from ventures that aren't financially viable. I rarely see someone take their own medicine, though – thus my enduring skepticism of the business plan.

That said, business plans are still the gateway to the world of venture capital. You can't get financing without a business plan, so in that case, a business plan is a mandatory part of the process. I haven't spent much time on venture capital in this book because I've been writing about "freeing yourself from corporate America."

In the first chapter, I contrasted the difference between lifestyle entrepreneurs and Bill Gates entrepreneurs, noting that this book is focused on the former. There's nothing wrong with launching the next great American company, but you're not likely to free yourself from corporate America by following that model.

Becoming the founder and CEO of a major American company is beyond the scope of this book. Those kinds of startups typically require large-scale venture capital at some early phase. This book works better for "fund as you go" businesses that are not intended to go through the process of becoming a publicly-traded company – a common end goal for most venture capital scenarios.

I've never seen a venture capital scenario firsthand that worked out well for a business. True, you can look to today's business pages and find some that did, and in a big way. But it's a high stakes game. I'm referring less to the pressures of big-time financing, and more about losing control of your vision. I've seen venture capitalists alter businesses beyond recognition. And I've seen owners lose control to investment vultures and literally bawl with remorse. The old saw, "be careful who you get into bed with," could have been invented for venture capitalists.

Some people are drawn to venture capital because it's glamorous. When good-looking people in power suits fly to your company to talk smack, things do seem pretty swell. If you go the venture capital route, just make sure you are clear about the amount of ownership you are going to have and what the downside might be. Make sure the money folks are either going to step out of the way, or be true partners who share your vision and strategy.

In the end, venture capital is just one form of financing. There are always other options. I tend to be a bigger fan of debt financing or business loans. Loans and credit lines give you a cash influx but more control over business direction.

Multi-level marketing (MLM) is another topic that comes up when people look at business startups. One of the biggest appeals of MLM is that a legit MLM operation gives you a head start with a pre-defined product or service. Some businesses would be offended if you labeled them as MLM, for example Avon. This is a good sign. Only worthwhile MLM companies would object to the label. Needless to say, most MLM ventures are either cults or wobbly pyramid schemes that should be avoided like we used to avoid bad school lunches. Once MLM types start talking to you about "building your downline," it's time to run for cover.

But if an MLM is focused on selling products and getting commissions, and if it doesn't require a hefty down payment on your part, then it may be an option. MLM can provide a useful sales and marketing education, but it's also a too-easy way out from developing your own materials and ideas.

Franchises are a similar concept. If you buy into a franchise, you get the benefit of the umbrella company's products and marketing. There are franchises in almost every industry. For example, you can buy into a home inspection franchise and get the credibility of being affiliated with a bigger company. Of course, you give up a decent chunk of money in exchange for that credibility.

I don't have a one-size-fits-all opinion on buying into a franchise. It can be a good option for folks who are looking to get something off the ground, have a bit of money saved, and have a passion for a business concept that already exists. Some franchises give you a lot of leeway to define how your business will look and run. Others do not. I tend to lean toward inventing your business rather than buying into somebody else's, but there is a time and a place for franchises.

Another way to look at franchises is to flip the concept on its head: roll out your own business as if it might someday be a franchise. To some people, that's a repugnant idea, and to me, I guess it is too. I would never do a "Jon Reed's Beef Stew for the Soul" book series. Franchises can be financially powerful, but they are also limiting. However, it doesn't hurt to think about the re-usability (or scalability) of your ideas.

Whenever you can increase revenues for your business exponentially while increasing costs only incrementally, that's a sign you have a winning business model. To me, that's what scalability is all about: serving larger markets while keeping costs under control. In franchising terms, moving beyond one location can also be a key to streamlining your costs through volume, and therefore having a more competitive business model.

It's important to understand why franchising works even if we make a conscious decision not to take that route. We can still apply the lessons of franchising to our own ventures. The strength of franchising is its out-of-the-box processes and systems. Anyone in business can learn from these techniques. The more teachable and scalable our venture is, the better our chances.

If you're like me, you're more interested in maintaining control of your ideas, lifestyle and values than losing all of those things in exchange for becoming a picture on the wall of a company you no longer control. Assuming you place the high value on creative control that I do, I recommend keeping the options of venture capital, MLM, and franchises at arm's length.

And if you must do a business plan, don't waste months on it. If writing a plan gets you off the couch, then by all means, do the plan. Just remember that when the plan is done, the business is exactly what it was before you started – a good idea in dire need of execution. And good execution is a lot harder than coming up with a good idea. Business planning is oxymoronic, because there's no real way to plan for business, any more than there is to plan for life.

A good plan might help you to sleep better at night, but there are gotchas on the way that you didn't and couldn't predict. The ability (and willingness) to adjust your venture on the fly to meet market demands is a lot more important than a pretty plan full of seductive Excel formulas.

That said, number crunching is still vital to a successful business. It's just as vital to personal finance. But the best numbers are not hypothetical business plan numbers, but real ones, certified by our own sweat. In the next section, we'll look at how to use "real numbers" to our advantage.

"Life isn't worth much without dreams, and the bigger the dream, the bigger the financing behind it."

Gut Check #4: Making the Money We Earn Count

I never said this was the easy way. I wouldn't have written this book if I wasn't convinced that in the long run, it's a lot better to put assets to work for you. In the short term, however, the going tends to get harder. But unlike the bad jobs I have endured, I've never regretted the choices I've made along the path this book outlines. I doubt you will either. At the same time, we're not doing this just for fun. It's not easy to generate reliable cash flow – that's why it's so important to make the money from our new ventures count.

At this point in the book, we have a handle on how to brand ourselves and how to approach our current employment. We understand the importance of developing a marketable expertise, but we recognize that becoming a billable expert has its limitations. If we don't want to be servants to a paycheck, we need more than expertise: we need the flexibility that income-generating assets can provide.

We've looked at how to create those assets and how to take them to the marketplace. If things go well, we'll generate some income from those assets. But there's some pretty alarming news: that income is not going to help us unless we become a lot better about managing money.

Some people have the same bias towards financial management that they do towards sales. They feel it's not for them, that they are somehow a sellout if they attempt to learn how money works. Or they have "enough to get by," so there's no need to take their financial skills further. I hope by now we've poked enough holes in that kind of thinking, because getting by is not going to get us off the hamster wheel.

Believing that "money is evil" while working 9 to 5 within a market economy is one of the most self-defeating approaches to modern life. Money is a tool and a method of exchange. It is also our economy's means, for better and often for worse, of assigning relative market value to different assets and professions.

We can bemoan those circumstances if we want, but I wonder how beneficial such tirades are when the keys to improving our circumstance are right there in front of us, if we can just get over ourselves and start accepting proper payment in exchange for our best work. Accumulating financial resources is not the crime – it's what most people *do* with those resources that tends to disappoint. But we can't ignore the power of applied wealth for solving problems that can't be addressed by living in a state of broke resentment.

On the other hand, I do not object to the phrase "I have enough." Finding the right level of material comfort without giving in to the slick temptations of gadget culture is a big piece of the puzzle. But whatever that level is, "enough" won't feel like much if we find ourselves jobless and our skills outdated. Thus the need for income-generating assets, and the need to manage that income effectively. Life isn't worth much without dreams, and the bigger the dream, the bigger the financing behind it.

In the next section, we'll take a fresh look at personal finance through the lens of the financial statements that businesses use – but with a different view of what constitutes a real asset.

Part VII:

Financing Your Business of One

We Are a Business of One

Reckoning With Your Balance Sheet

Budgeting Stinks – So What's the Alternative?

Plotting Our Freedom – How Can Number-Crunching Help Us?

"If we pour more money into a flawed structure, it's going to spill right through. The leaks must get plugged. Otherwise, our lifestyle will simply rise to meet the level of income."

We Are a Business of One

Money is elusive. It doesn't matter how much you make if it leaks out the back of your life. We can't be free from pink slip culture unless we know how to maximize the power of our existing income while diversifying our revenue sources. The starting point? Tune out the money management pundits and think about finance like a business does.

It's not accurate to grade our financial health in terms of isolated factors, such as a paid-off mortgage or a fat salary. Some of the wealthiest people I know don't make much money, but they sure know how not to spend it. The smartest way to approach our finances is to view ourselves as a business of one (those who are married or seriously co-habitating can expand that to two).

The Business of One encompasses everything: what we bank, what we spend, what we invest, and what we blow. As a business of one, we can self-analyze by using the same financial statements businesses do: the cash flow statement, the profit and loss, and the balance sheet. It's rare to be strong across the board. Usually there is a disconnect or a leak somewhere.

You don't plug those leaks by budgeting. People who sweat every expense should stop surveying the damage and focus on revenues. That said, I *am* a huge fan of online banking, because your transactions can be easily pulled into financial statements. When receipts are stuffed in shoeboxes, you can't do much analysis.

When you download your transactions, you're confronted with revealing facts about how much you burn. And if you're using accounting software like Quicken, you can quickly calculate your net worth also. Many of us have a negative net worth – part of being an American is putting flat screens ahead of our kids' education fund. That negative net worth is not just the result of being overworked and underpaid. Often, poor financial habits are to blame, and bad financial habits lead to a bad financial structure.

If we pour more money into a flawed structure, it's going to spill right through. The leaks must get plugged. Otherwise, our lifestyle will simply rise to meet the level of income. But with some financial smarts, we can avoid "lifestyle creep." We can get that knowledge by learning how businesses keep the lights on.

Businesses have a better handle on finance than individuals for two reasons: first, businesses tend to be less emotional about money. They are less likely to waste it on poor decisions and pricey indulgences. And since businesses literally go under without proper financial management, their analytical tools have to be more sophisticated.

This section of the book is a bit different than the others. Up to this point, every chapter was a self-contained concept. In the next chapters, I go into the guts of financial management. I recommend you read the entire section as a whole.

Depending on where you're at with your finances, you might want to skim or skip over this section. On the other hand, if you want to take a fresh look at personal finance from a perspective you may not have seen before, then this section is for you. When we're done, we'll have a clearer sense of how the cash flow from our assets can help us.

"Since I have an absurd emotional attachment to my car, I'm not allowed to list it as an asset, even though it's paid off. A paid-off car is a good thing, but since I would never sell it, I don't get to list it on my balance sheet."

Reckoning With Your Balance Sheet

A balance sheet can be a terrible thing to behold, so we save ourselves the trouble either by not creating one, or doing it casually. Unfortunately, listing our home as an asset and patting ourselves on the back is not going to get it done.

A properly constructed balance sheet tallies up the resources we have to throw at our problems. This could be the difference between leaving a frustrating job tomorrow versus having to dig in with a long-term exit plan. You can't walk away if you don't know what you're working with.

The easiest way to generate a balance sheet is through an accounting program, but that won't get you the kind of balance sheet we're after. The best way to make ours is with a spreadsheet like Excel. It doesn't take much to put together a simple two-column spreadsheet with liabilities on one side and assets on the other. A piece of paper might serve even better than fancy software. That's because a full-featured accounting program might classify some things as "assets" that are not. And it won't take into account other personal goods that may indeed be assets.

Financial advisors promise that your home and retirement account are assets. For the purposes of this book, they may not be. When you do your *Free From Corporate America* balance sheet, you only list assets that can be converted into cash in a short-term timeframe (three to six months max). Retirement accounts can only be included if you are willing to liquidate them.

Most people are not, and for good reason. So for our balance sheet, you can only include your retirement account if you really are willing to pull the money out now. Of course, you must subtract any penalties and early withdrawal fees and list only the remainder of your IRA as an asset.

The reason we keep these "assets" at a distance is because in this book, we're not waiting until retirement to turn this ship around. When it comes to freeing ourselves from corporate America, cash is paramount. Extra funds can be applied in compelling ways: we can step back from our careers and pursue a more promising field; we can launch a new side venture, or we can shift to part-time work and pursue our own projects aggressively. You can't make those choices without an accurate balance sheet.

We approach the balance sheet differently in this book because our premise is different: we no longer believe that 9 to 5 living is going to get us there. Therefore, we're going to stop putting all our cash into inaccessible IRAs and use at least some of it to fund the creation of our own income-generating assets. These assets will give us a "home run potential" we didn't have before, and they will increase our job satisfaction as we get closer to working on our own terms.

With that in mind, what do you do with your home on our balance sheet? If you own your home, you may have been advised to list the entire worth of the home as an asset on your balance sheet and then list what you haven't paid on the mortgage as a liability. Since we are primarily interested in cash we can use in the short-term, we don't do that.

On this book's balance sheet, there are two ways to account for the value of your home: if you have enough equity that you could refinance your primary mortgage and take money out, then list the amount of money you could pull out as an asset. (Strictly speaking, refinance money is a loan, not an asset, but since it's protected by the underlying value of the house, we are bending the rules.)

Alternately, if you could sell your home and make a profit, and *if* you have no problem selling your home and cashing out, then you can list your home as an asset. If you go this route, you need to determine the price of the new home you would buy when you sell your old one, and then determine the cost of the down payment on the new home. Take the profit you would make from the sale of your old home, deduct the cost of the new down payment, and you have the true amount of your home as an asset for our purposes. It's not as complicated as it sounds: we are simply looking for the cash you would really have to work with if you sold your home, and nothing else.

Yep, this is a more exacting process than a typical balance sheet. You're certainly encouraged to do a more conventional balance sheet alongside this one. By taking this strict stance, I'm not saying you shouldn't put any more money into your home or your IRA. But you're going to need some capital outside of those investments (unless you are able to borrow against them in a way that is financially appealing).

Using our balance sheet, how do you treat your car? Similarly to your house. If your car is paid off, take the resale value of your car, subtract the cost of the next car you would buy, and list the difference as your automobile asset. You may wonder why we aren't allowed to simply subtract the new car's down payment as we did with the home. The answer: financing a car is not so terrific. Financing a home gives you access to home equity loans and competitive interest rates (not to mention tax deductions). Since car loans do not provide these benefits, the total cost of the new car, not just the down payment, must be subtracted from the value of our current car.

I have a car problem. My car is probably worth $14,000. I could buy a used car for less and pocket the difference. But since I have an absurd emotional attachment to my car, I'm not allowed to list it as an asset, even though it's paid off. A paid-off car is a good thing, and it could certainly help me out in an emergency cash crunch, but since I would otherwise never sell it, I don't get to list it on my balance sheet. You can only list a paid-off car as an asset if you're willing to sell it to get a new venture off the ground.

The benefit of a paid-off car will become apparent in our next chapter, when we construct our monthly cash flow statement. But my attachment to my car is a great illustration of how "assets" can get us into trouble, and how we have to be careful about classifying them as assets if we have no intention of ever selling them. No, my paid off car is not a liability. But it's not a brilliant financial investment either.

So what else constitutes an asset? Besides our checking and savings accounts, not much. It *is* possible to classify businesses with proven income streams as assets, but following this book's rules, unless you're willing to sell those assets (and could liquidate them quickly), they don't qualify here. (Note that this type of business is still a good thing even if it doesn't show up on our balance sheet. We will account for it in our cash flow and profit and loss statements.)

Some books, including the classic *Your Money or Your Life*, tell you to count material possessions as assets if they can be converted into cash. I don't agree – unless you are truly ready to part with them. Extreme example: a wedding ring. I don't consider it an asset because it would only be sold in dire times. By the time you're selling your wedding ring, you have more to worry about than corporate America.

The problem with listing our possessions as assets is that in reality, we're not likely to part with them. My DVD and CD collections are probably worth $1000 in cash (and weren't a great investment to begin with), but there's only a handful I would sell – bad gifts like *The Mummy Returns* come to mind. Either way, *The Mummy Returns* isn't going to transform my balance sheet.

Since I wouldn't freely sell my DVDs, they do not qualify for this book's balance sheet. The same is true of collectibles. Those who want to include the net worth of their figurine collections must be willing to sell those collections on the spot. Most collectors would rather live on dog biscuits, so their collections will not be included on our financial statements.

By contrast, I have a friend who is a freelance writer. She has techy bling like iPods lying around – stuff she was given for product reviews. I consider those things assets because she has no attachment to them. For this book, if you're not willing to put it up on eBay this weekend, you can't list it as an asset. Yes, maybe they are part of some last resort safety net, but this book is about building ourselves up so we don't ever have to face such times. With these principles in mind, the end result of our asset column might look something like this (I'll use small numbers for easy math):

Checking:	$100
Savings:	$250
House:	$500
Car:	$200
Household Items (CDs, TV, etc.):	$100
Total Assets:	$1,150

Then we move on to liabilities. For most of us, the liabilities column is not a pretty picture. Typically, credit card debt alone is enough to earn us at least 5K in liabilities. If we owe money to friends, family, or our alma mater, that also goes on the liabilities column. That last one burns, since we can't list our degrees as an asset.

The good news about this book's system? If we owe money on a house, boat, or car, we don't have to list it as a liability here, since we didn't list it as an asset. As long as the resale value of the asset is greater than the amount we owe, it doesn't have to be included as a liability here. If we owe more on something than its worth, then we *do* have to list it (one not-so-fun example: payments still due on a car that has been totaled in an accident).

Unless we own some bad-luck floodlands, we should be able to avoid listing any financed items as liabilities. One thing we're not getting into here: businesses make distinctions between short-term and long-term liabilities to get a clearer picture of when the hammer comes down for particular debts. You can do this if you want, but it's not essential to our purposes.

A simple liabilities list might look like this:

Credit Card A:	$500
Credit Card B:	$300
Family Loan:	$200
Student Loan:	$200
Total Liabilities:	$1,200

(If you only have $1,200 in liabilities, you are looking better than most of your neighbors, even the ones who drive nice-looking cars.)

Once we've added up our assets and liabilities, we can subtract one from the other to determine our "net worth." In this case, our net worth is a negative $50. Worry not. It is quite common to start out with a negative net worth using this rigid method, given we have excluded retirement accounts and homes that could balance the equation in our favor.

Homes and IRAs make a balance sheet look pretty, but that optimistic type of balance sheet is deceptive, as the value we are listing for our home and retirement account is not usually something we can turn to in order to solve the work predicaments that are the focus of this book.

My own balance sheet isn't going to win any kudos on Wall Street, thought it's headed in a good direction. My liabilities, which are too demoralizing to include here, involve a modest (but annoying) amount of consumer debt, as well as a business credit line with a balance outstanding.

I have also self-financed the development of several assets, which has drained some of the available cash from my balance sheet. I have two books out; this one is my third, and there are two more on the way. I can't list them as assets, because at this time I can't (and wouldn't) sell them, but one of the books is generating some decent income, so hopefully more good news is to come.

You may experience a similar dip in your balance sheet as you get new ventures off the ground, but that is the kind of risk you have to take if you want to keep dreams alive and give your life a serious upside. My books give me a focus for my future. You can't put a price on charting a way forward that inspires and motivates you.

Constructing this kind of balance sheet is strong medicine. As we come clean on our numbers, we can see how credit cards and other shortcuts prop up our lifestyles. It's important that we don't blame ourselves if the picture doesn't look pretty at first. Many of us have encountered expenses that were beyond what our income could handle, and we can't get down on ourselves for falling into debt to keep ourselves going. Beating ourselves up is not the point of this exercise at all.

But if we can find a way to suck it up and return to this balance sheet regularly in order to assess our progress, we can turn our situation around and build on our success. If for some reason we go in the other direction and acquire more debt, the balance sheet will be the place where the pileup becomes obvious. But with the right tactics in place, the chances are decent that we will start to see some improvements in our balance sheet as debts decrease and assets increase. Even small shifts can have a huge impact on our options.

You may have heard of that investment rule: "pay yourself first." (This rule refers to the practice of putting money in retirement accounts before you pay any other bills.) My variation on that rule is: "fund yourself first." No matter how tight the cash is, make sure those projects are moving ahead one way or the other. Put in money, put in time; put in both if you can. If you live strategically and not just paycheck-to-paycheck, chances are good that your balance sheet will eventually reflect the wisdom of your approach.

"The point is not to live like saints, but to draw connections between our TGIF nights on one side and our dependency on corporate employment on the other."

Budgeting Stinks – So What's the Alternative?

Budgeting is tedious. Yet that do-good voice in our head scolds us when we don't do it. My biggest beef: budgeting pounds into your head that your income is fixed. For the budgeter, expenses are the enemy, weeds everywhere, always threatening to wreck the financial scenery. But here's the problem: to claim a lasting victory over the mounting costs of life, you must boost revenues. Managing expenses is part of it, but "budgeting" promotes a feeling of scarcity and uptight self-management.

That said, you *do* have to understand how money liberates itself from your wallet. You're not getting out of the cubicle without that. So what's the alternative to budgets? Use the same kinds of financial statements businesses do.

We've already talked about the balance sheet, which is a snapshot of the overall financial picture. Now we can consider the usefulness of two more tools: the cash flow statement and the income (or profit and loss) statement, which is a component of the cash flow statement.

In the process of compiling the data for these statements, you solve the budgeting problem. The most efficient way to do this is with accounting software. If you download your transactions into that software regularly, you will have all the data you need to crunch some pretty impressive numbers. OK, the numbers themselves may not impress – at least initially – but you can track them over time, and hopefully they will become impressive.

The software you choose doesn't really matter, but I download all my personal transactions into Quicken. I also download my credit card expenses there. When you have all your data in one place, you can do some realistic forecasting. It's very hard to project forward by looking at last month's bank statement, because there are too many costs (like car repair) that don't fall within that timeframe.

But once you extend that horizon a year or longer, you can make an accurate calculation of your typical monthly expenses. With a bit of extra energy, you can even classify each expense into a relevant category. But what we're really after is a clear view of what our total monthly costs are.

Let's say you have three years' worth of data in an accounting program. The hard part is getting the data in there – regular downloads are the key. Once the data is in, you can generate a report that shows your total expenses over a three-year period. Divide that total by 36, and you have a real working total of what it costs you to live month to month. And since it's based on three years of numbers, you've taken into account all the incidentals, all the pizza deliveries, all the flat tires, all the unanticipated snafus.

Super old-timers call this your "nut," as in: "If I don't earn five grand a month, I won't be able to make my nut." Your nut is a valuable piece of information, and in the age of credit cards and home equity lines, that's a hard number to get a handle on – it's too easy to conceal your expenses during a refinance by burying them under borrowed cash.

For some, calculating our "nut" is a pretty trying exercise. We want to believe we live on less than we actually do. But over three years, we can see how vacations and digital cameras and wedding presents add up. And we see it much more accurately than we would with a wishful thinking budget that doesn't account for our penchant for a nice bottle of wine. Once you have those costs calculated, the goal is to streamline them so you can enhance your lifestyle's profit margin.

There are some obvious things you can do to reduce that monthly cost level. You can pay off high-interest credit cards (a wise first step), or you can get out from under a car loan. Beyond the debt service, there may be other ways to scrimp and save. If we take the extra step of categorizing our expenses, we will spot spending trends.

For example, if you classify all the DVDs you buy into their own category, you might be shocked enough by the grand total to Netflix them instead. I'm always amazed by my compulsion to own DVDs I rarely watch again. Over a three-year period, you can see the price of collecting "stuff" more clearly. That can firm your all-important resolve.

My expenses have a tendency to rise to my level of income. This is typical, and *not* what we are going for. We are shooting for real profitability each year, excess cash we can invest in the creation of assets, or, alternately, put into income-generating accounts. Boosting revenues is important, but profitability – the difference between our monthly revenues and expenses – is the real key.

When you force yourself to go through your downloads each month, it's not hard to identify the areas you binge on. Bingeing is part of life, but it's good to remember the point of the book *Your Money or Your Life*: we use our money to buy time (life energy), so when we spend money recklessly, we are essentially handcuffing ourselves to our desks, ensuring we will have to slog through our jobs at whatever hourly rate we command. The lower our salaries, the more costly our indulgences are.

As we accumulate wealth, we can get away with more carefree spending, though it's still important to track it. But when we are trying to break free from the cycle of bad jobs and bad debt, our margin for error is tight, and we pay dearly for our indulgences. The point is not to live like saints, but to draw connections between our "TGIF nights" on one side and our dependency on corporate employment on the other.

Looking for income and expense trends is similar to how businesses build a cash flow statement. A statement of cash flow totals up the income from all of our revenue sources (work, investments, repaid loans, etc.), subtracts all the expenses from that same period (business expenses, personal expenses, debt service, etc.) and shows us a gain or loss in cash flows over the period we are looking at.

It's rare to see a cash flow statement geared for individuals, but some software programs will generate them, and if not, you can easily make your own on paper or via a spreadsheet. It's important to revisit the statement each year (or quarter) to spot overall trends.

A simple cash flow statement, appropriated for personal finance, might look something like this:

JR'S CASH FLOW STATEMENT
(for the period 8/1/07-8/1/08)

Net Income from Operations (Business):	$60,000
Net Income from non-IRA Investments:	$250
Net Income from Rental Properties:	$10,000
Total Personal Expenses:	($65,000)
Beginning Period Cash:	$10,000
Ending Period Cash:	$15,250

So, using this simplistic (and fictionalized) view of my cash flow, what we see is that my business made a net profit of $60,000 after expenses (that's what the "net" means), plus I had $10,000 in rental income (also after expenses) and $250 in investment income (remember, using our asset rules, I am only counting non-retirement investment income on this statement). So I have three income sources going into my bank account, but then I have outgoing expenses of 65K (the parenthetical indicates this is in fact a negative number for our purposes).

So what we have is a net gain in cash flow of $5,250 from the beginning of the year to the end. You can break out the cash flow statement in more detail if you want a closer look at how each line item was calculated. For example, your cash flow statement might indicate total wages and then indicate taxes as one expense subtotal, so that you can see how much tax you pay on your salary each year. A more complex form of the cash flow statement (for a business) can be found on wikipedia.org, using the search phrase "cash flow statement."

As for the income/"profit and loss" statement, businesses consider that part of an overall cash flow statement. An income statement is a closer look at an operational piece of business and whether that business made or lost money. An income statement might include investment income or business rental income, but those other sources of income would likely be itemized separately, enabling the finance team to assess the actual revenues and expenses related to the core products and services of that business.

Therefore, the "net income from operations" line on our sample cash flow statement is taken directly from a companion profit and loss statement. Behind that line item is a complex story of all the revenues my business brought in, minus all the expenses, which brought me to that net income from operations number of $60,000.

So the summary cash flow statement deals with all those business interactions in one basic line that says:

Net Income from Operations (Business): $60,000

For my sample cash flow statement, the companion income statement would be a closer look at how I arrived at $60K in net business income, looking at each expense category and adding them together to compare against revenues. Sometimes income statements are done on an "accrual" basis, which means the statement is based on when sales are booked. Using an accrual method, money we have invoiced but not yet collected is considered revenue. For our purposes here, we're sticking with a cash-based income statement.

A summary income statement might look like this:

JR's INCOME STATEMENT FOR HIS 'S' CORPORATION
for the period 8/1/07 – 8/1/08)

<u>Revenues</u>

Client A:	$125,000
Client B:	$4,500
Interest Income:	$500
Total Revenue:	$130,000

<u>Expenses</u>

Client A:	$37,000
Client B:	$3,000

Total Expenses:	$40,000
Income, Pre-Tax:	$90,000
Income Taxes:	($30,000)
Net Income:	$60,000

Note that the net income of $60K now plugs into my previous cash flow statement. In my case, income taxes would not actually be included on the expense line of the business income statement as my business income is taxed only at the personal level, but I included them for our purposes here.

Income statements are often most useful in a detailed version. That's because it's eye opening to see what we spent on different areas of a business and where the bulk of our revenues came from. There's not room in this book for a detailed income statement, but you can get an idea of how you would break out the categories into further detail from the example above. Many software programs will break them out for you further.

Another thing to keep in mind from my example: I like to measure my expenses against a particular client to determine the profitability of that client, but most income statements would divide expenses up into categories like "Cost of Goods Sold," "Marketing Expenses," and "Administrative Expenses." There's more than one way to go here; the key is having a summary income statement that you can also drill into when you need specific detail on each type of income or expense (such as being able to compare cellular and land line phone expenses).

So how can we use these statements to improve our financial picture? The income statement is useful for a focused look at a particular venture. For example, I use QuickBooks to track my business expenses and earnings. Within QuickBooks, I have classified my expenses and revenues into different projects, so I can calculate the profit (or loss) of particular ventures. It is worth mentioning that this kind of income and expense detail is also required if/when you consider the option of outside investors or financing. Plus it's a beautiful thing to have come tax time.

On the previous summary income statement, what we know is that I made a $60,000 profit, but within QuickBooks, I can check the profitability of various aspects of my business revenues that combined to total 60K. Within QuickBooks, I have classified my revenues and expenses into different "classes." For example, I can look at how much profit I have made on my SAP consulting book after deducting the promotional expenses from the revenues.

I can do the same for *Resumes From Hell*, or any other aspect of my business. I can run a similar income statement for my business as a whole. You might choose to run a side venture at a financial loss for a period of time, but it's still important to see exactly how much you are making (or losing) on each venture you launch. This helps to focus on profitability and figure out which business ventures aren't viable. Since our focus is on freeing up our time, we want to head to the areas where the level of profit is highest compared to our time spent. Crunching the numbers can show us the way.

If I run the numbers on *Resumes From Hell*, I can see that I have lost money so far. It is not a profitable venture because our marketing campaigns have been expensive. Every time we market the book, we get excellent coverage and our book sales jump, but not enough to offset the marketing expense.

This data factors heavily into future decisions. For example, for future *Resumes From Hell* campaigns, we could decide to forego traditional marketing and spend more time and resources on Internet-based marketing, which tends to be cheaper than direct mail or cold calling.

As I mentioned, there are times in business when you don't mind losing money or keeping a break-even venture afloat. In the case of *Resumes From Hell*, we are going to write a companion book called *Resumes From Heaven* that we think will raise the sales of both titles. The visibility we've gained from doing radio and television spots also has a value, not to mention the experience we have gained.

But we do need to pay attention to what the numbers tell us, and an income statement can help you hone in on a particular venture. The cash flow statement, on the other hand, has a broader purpose. Your accounting software gathers all the material you need for a cash flow statement. In Quicken, for example, I can see all of my account balances, either cash or credit card. I can also see all my revenues. I can see how much I made (or lost) from my business, which shows up in the form of monthly paychecks or cash distributions in my deposit column. I can also see how much I made from investment income. All the sources on a statement of cash flows can be similarly tracked.

The cash flow statement shows us some important things – especially when we compare it to the statements of previous years and quarters. We may be struck by how our income from investments (or a side business) has increased from year to year. For example, we might find that a year ago, income from our side ventures comprised 10 percent of our total income, and our work salary was the other 90 percent. This year, it might be 20 percent from side ventures and 80 percent from our 9 to 5.

That's a positive trend we can take from the cash flow numbers. If that number from the side venture keeps going up, we can look to make a move to part-time work or leave our job entirely.

It's important to note that we also need the balance sheet to tell the whole story. For example, we might have racked up debt on a credit card but not made payments on that card. Depending on how we run the numbers, that debt might not show up on the income statement. If we only count expenses coming from our bank account, those credit card underpayments would hide our true expense total.

Here's how credit card debt can slip by us: let's say we put a $3,000 family vacation on a credit card, but we only paid the minimum $25 balance on the credit card each month. That means we only spent $300 on the vacation that year. Unless we make a point of importing all our credit card charges into our accounting program, all we may see in the check register in terms of vacation expenses is that $300.

Therefore, if we pretend for a moment that I had taken this type of vacation, the cash flow statement I printed earlier was as follows:

Net Income from Operations (Business):	$60,000
Net Income from Investments:	$250
Net Income from Rental Properties:	$10,000
Total Personal Expenses:	($65,000)
Beginning Period Cash:	$10,000
Ending Period Cash:	$15,250

We can assume that the $300 for the vacation was part of the total personal expenses that I paid of $65,000. But the rest of that $3,000 vacation expense ($2,700 to be precise) may not be incorporated into this statement. After all, the cash flow statement does not track overall increases in assets and liabilities beyond cash on hand. So we have an illusion here on the cash flow statement. It says that our cash for the year went up to $15,250, but that gain in cash flow is not much help if our credit card balances also went up.

So we might miss that on our cash flow statement, but the balance sheet would show us whether our consumer debt increased or decreased from year to year. So if we see that our cash on hand has increased by $5,000 on the balance sheet, but our credit card debts have increased by a similar number, we haven't actually progressed.

The balance sheet can give us some great summary numbers and catch any cash flow illusions, but we need all three reports to assess profitability and cash on hand, digging into as much detail as we might want.

Of course, the increase in cash flow noted on our cash flow statement also ties into our balance sheet, where we would list our total cash on hand as an asset. It's just important to remember that the cash we are concerned with on our balance sheet is "after tax" cash that we have already paid taxes on.

Cash being held in a business account is a different kind of asset, because that money has not yet been taxed, and we may have to split some of that cash with a business partner. Being clear about after-tax income is very important. It helps us to realize that our after-tax disposable income is extremely valuable because of all the hoops we have jumped through and the dues we have paid on the income in order to get it into our checking account where we can now invest it.

So for our purposes, "cash on hand" in a business is not part of our personal balance sheet. With that in mind, let's revisit the balance sheet we used in the prior chapter and link it with our cash flow statement. Then we'll see how we spotted the problem with the credit card vacation.

Although the checking account balance in my original balance sheet example was only $100, we're going to change it now to include the proper number from our cash flow statement.

Remember that our cash flow example was:

Net Income from Operations (Business):	$60,000
Net Income from Investments:	$250
Net Income from Rental Properties:	$10,000
Total Personal Expenses:	($65,000)
Beginning Period Cash:	$10,000
Ending Period Cash:	$15,250

So, our cash on hand number of $15,250 should be similar (or exact) to the total number from our checking and savings account total from the balance sheet.

Let's alter the numbers in our imaginary balance sheet so that they add up properly.

The original assets list from the last chapter looked like this:

Checking:	$100
Savings:	$250
House:	$500
Car:	$200
Household Items (CDs, TV, etc):	$100
Total Assets:	$1,150

Now, let's take that original assets section and alter it to fit our current example of the cash flow statement, where we listed $15,250 as our ending period cash. This should be very close (or equal) to our cash on hand in our checking and savings accounts:

Checking:	$15,000
Savings:	$250

House:	$500
Car:	$200
Household Items (CDs, TV, etc):	$100
Total Assets:	$16,050

Note that all I have done here is added money to our checking and savings from our original balance sheet so I can repurpose it for this example and have the total of the checking and savings add up to $15,250. The statements should always tie in together and cross-check each other. In real life, of course, we can't alter our numbers – we have to live with them. But our actual numbers should still match up on all three statements.

In this case, we can see that the checking/savings total of $15,250 is an exact match with our "cash on hand" number from our cash flow statement. That is what we are looking for. We now have a tight connection between these two documents.

However, there is a problem – the matter of our $3,000 vacation. Right now our cash flow is artificially strong. We need the liabilities section of the balance sheet to bring that issue to light.

That's easily done. Let's take my original liabilities section and alter it slightly to fit our current example.

The original looked like this:

Credit Card A:	$500
Credit Card B:	$300
Family Loan:	$200
Student Loan:	$200
Total Liabilities:	$1,200

Let's now add in the unpaid $2,700 portion of the vacation to Credit Card A:

Credit Card A:	$3,200 ($500 plus the $2,700)
Credit Card B:	$300
Family Loan:	$200
Student Loan:	$200
Total Liabilities	$3,900

So the balance sheet showed us something the cash flow statement didn't. It's nice that we have $15,250 on hand in cash, but we do carry $3,900 in liabilities, including $3,500 in credit card debt. In this example, our net worth is $12,150 (Total Assets minus Total Liabilities, or $16,050 minus $3,900). That's not the worst situation by any means, but it's a different story than the cash flow statement told us.

Taken together, these financial statements give us an objective view – often disappointing at first – of where we stand. But the sting goes away when we realize how much these statements can help us leave financial insecurity behind. The best part is yet to come: we can use the cash flow statement to calculate how soon we can retire or make a shift to part-time work. I'll cover that in my next chapter.

"When my book income matches my 'monthly nut,' I have hit my walk-away number. I now have the option to fire my clients."

Plotting Our Freedom – How Can Number Crunching Help Us?

If we're going to beat the system, we need some home runs. We'll do that by owning marketable assets, but as we've said, those assets won't mean anything if we don't have a comfort level with financial management.

Crunching numbers is how we identify which of our projects are profitable. It's also how we spot self-defeating leaks in our spending. Money means a lot more when we realize it's the difference between a self-created life on our terms and a long-term tour of duty in low-ceiling middle management.

With that motivation in mind, let's see how we can take the data from these financial statements we took the trouble to compile and apply them to our situation. As we do, we're looking for key trends that can help us make adjustments. Businesses sometimes call these indicators "metrics."

Here are some numbers and metrics that have big implications:

"Asset Income" Metric: What percentage of our income comes from areas other than our jobs? What is the improvement in that percentage of our income from year to year?

Obviously, the higher that percentage is, the better off we are. The less we need our jobs, the more we stand to get out of them.

Of course, we can calculate this percentage directly from our cash flow statement without fancy calculations. All we have to do is compare them from year to year and chart our progress.

"Monthly Nut"/Walk-Away Metric: What is our "monthly nut"? How much do we really need every month for our expenses? And how much would it take to "walk away"?

We have already calculated the monthly nut number in the "Budgeting Stinks" chapter. But we haven't made full use of it. *The "monthly nut" also serves as our "walk away" number*, as in: How much do we need to earn each month in order to walk away from our jobs?

Example: when/if my book income matches my "monthly nut," I have hit my walk away number.

At that point, I have the option of "firing" my clients and concentrating solely on my own books. Or I could keep my clients. But my flexibility on how my daily time is spent just changed dramatically, and as we've noted, control over time is the key determinant of success in the time-as-commodity era. Not having to work 9 to 5 frees us up to pursue our true vocation, build powerful assets, or both.

Often we have a series of walk-away numbers rather than just one. In my case, that first walk away number is not the ultimate number – I will still have to work to promote my books and maintain that income stream. But from that point forward, I don't have to put up with much client BS. So the "monthly nut" is a number we can use to decide: (a) when we can walk away from jobs to focus on our own income-generating projects or (b) when we can walk away completely and live solely off investment or business income.

"Cash in the Bank": Once we establish our emergency fund, how much do we have left for our own ventures? And how much has that number grown from year to year?

The emergency fund is a tough call. I hear the phrase "six months in expenses" a lot. Sounds OK to me, though if I had waited until I had six months in living expenses stashed away before launching my side ventures, this book would not exist. So we might have to get by with a shorter-term emergency fund rather than the full six months. Whatever timeframe you decide upon, beyond that emergency fund lies the "venture fund."

"Venture Fund": This is the cash reserve you build up to finance your side ventures that is not set aside for emergency funds, vacations, etc. As noted, the scope of those ventures is up to you. You could buy into a business, start your own, or team up with a friend on a real estate purchase. You could even hire your (hopefully) brilliant sister to write a screenplay for you to market, or you could buy studio time for your buddy's band in exchange for a percentage of CD profits (be especially careful with that last one!).

Other self-investments from the Venture Fund might be more career-oriented, like enrolling in a certification program so you can break into a new field. When you consider these types of investments, a prime consideration will be whether you need an income stream now or whether you can wait for a cash payout later. Assets can either provide steady income, a big payout at a later date, or a combination of both. How long you are willing to wait for income depends on how much you have in the bank, how annoyed you are with your current employment, and how much you are paid for your trouble.

Combine the "Venture Fund" and "Walk Away" Numbers to Make Your Move: You can use your "venture fund number" to help you with your "walk away" plan. For example, let's say your employer presents you with an option to move from full-time to part-time work. If you switch to part-time, you'll have half days to devote to a new career or a new side business. But you'll need to make up the gap in income somehow. You can use your venture fund to fill that gap.

All you have to decide is how many months you need to cover before your side venture starts making money. Let's say that you arrive at an estimate of 12 months before the new pursuit starts generating cash flow. So in this case, you need a year's guaranteed income to make the move. If the income shift from full to part-time is $2,000 less a month, then $24,000 in cash will make up the difference. (This would likely be a bit less, depending on how your wages are taxed, since $2,000 in salary was not your net salary but your pre-tax salary before taxes. After taxes, it might have been more like $1,500 a month, which would be $18,000 saved.)

Therefore, once you have $18,000 in your Venture Fund, you can make your move. Obviously, having the cash to back up your plan doesn't eliminate the risk, but at least you have some idea of the timeframe you are gunning for. That's the difference between strategic risk and a hold-your-nose plunge. And you can always ramp up to full-time work on the other side if the part-time deal doesn't work out. At worst, you'll have a great adventure and some new skills to show for it.

It's good to remember there is also risk in not making the move. I talk with people like that all the time, fully aware they could find themselves on the same treadmill years later, or worse, led out to corporate pasture.

Risk Management Tradeoffs: You can minimize the risk of jumping ship by ensuring the number you need to live on each month is well-researched, as opposed to a hopeful estimate that doesn't take into account your contingencies. We've also talked about managing risk by carefully choosing which assets to develop, making sure to strike the best balance between what is marketable and where our passion lies.

I conducted an interesting experiment along these lines. Not long ago, I moved on from my biggest client. It was a great relationship in many ways, but it had become all-consuming. Now I have a new client that pays me quite a bit less per month, but in exchange, the demands on my time are significantly less also.

I did feel a strong breeze when I took this latest plunge, as the expenses will be more than a little tight for a while. The amount I am making is not currently enough to cover my "monthly nut" and business investments. You could say my financial boat has a slow leak right now.

But here's the good news: I am taking the extra time to finish this book and also the new SAP Web site I believe will eventually earn me a lot of income, in a market that has a proven demand and that I have good name recognition in. Best of all, it's the first SAP site I have owned myself. In the past, I have always built them for clients. This one will be my own asset.

To make things more appealing, the work I am doing for this new client is more strategic and is expanding my skills base. I will be able to use some of this new client work for my own site also, and I'll be able to "brand" both myself and them further in the market. So, I will be following several of the recommendations I have made in this book. If I can make it through this leaner revenue time, I'll emerge with greater market recognition, a more manageable work life, my own Web site, and new consulting skills. I expect revenues to catch up with my new skills and ventures accordingly.

These are the kinds of risk management tradeoffs you will weigh as you develop the tools to analyze your cash flow and figure out what kinds of assets you want to create. Of course, I will continue to work on my own "creative assets" such as this book and other fun projects still in the early stages. Over time, I hope to make the bulk of my money doing books like this one. These are long-term goals; I'll try to earn my way toward them.

You may have noticed that I didn't get into the "big retirement number" in this section. Most financial planning books focus on the million dollars or whatever figure we need to save in order to completely retire. That focus may be appropriate for fiftysomethings who are well on their way to socking away a million or more, and who are looking for advice on handling the final stages.

In this book, we're not concerning ourselves with that definitive retirement number. Why? *Because to make our first big move, we only need to come up with enough to live on for a finite period, such as a year.* Why wait till retirement to buy a JetStream we have become too nearsighted to drive?

If my research has shown me anything, it's that you don't have to be rich to be free in the sense we're gunning for here. To be "free," you need to be doing work that is pushing you towards your best self. And you need to be building assets that will give you the financial flexibility to choose when and how much to work.

Shooting for a million-dollar retirement number is not necessary to put these ideas in motion. Understanding how to make money work for you is crucial.

If I've accomplished anything in this book, I hope I've brought to light some "next step tactics" that can be used even when time is tight and circumstances are difficult. Most books of this kind preach only to those who already have the money to make new investments.

Here we are plotting a different way forward, one that is affordable enough for anyone to apply. The method outlined here might take elbow grease, but it's a proven winner. And like any approach that incorporates a bit of risk, it will bring some adventures along with it.

As for the financial statements, I take my own medicine each week. It's not always fun to run the numbers, especially during months when my debt goes up. But at other points, I can really see my progress. Those are the happy times, especially when you realize that the change in your financial state came from your own ideas and projects.

The Best Cash Management Tactics in Review

When we measure life on multiple factors, from cash flow to personal happiness, there are plenty of tradeoffs to consider. Sometimes a pricey vacation is essential even if it sets us back financially.

Now that we understand how financial statements can help us to plug leaks and chart our progress, let's review the cash management tactics that fit in with this book's approach:

• Live lean until you have the money to buy the time to do what you most want to do.

• Control expenses, but also strategically invest in yourself and your ventures.

• Spend time increasing revenues rather than seeing your income as "fixed." (When we see our income as fixed, we tend to fall into do-it-yourself mode, changing oil and clipping coupons as opposed to leveraging our greatest skills for higher income.)

• Use debt, including credit cards, only for emergencies and business financing (such as replacing the plumbing in a house we are about to sell). This is not an easy discipline.

• Use financial statements to track progress and set realistic goals from year to year.

• Maintain the best credit rating you can and make sure to use credit lines attached to your business and house (as opposed to personal credit cards) whenever possible. Don't be afraid to seize a business opportunity even it means taking on some debt. Strategic debt and consumer debt are different, though we should never be cavalier about any kind of debts.

• Plan for taxes and retirement, but don't run from good income opportunities just because that income will be taxed.

• Make sure that some of your savings is held outside of IRAs so you can invest it in new opportunities.

• Remember that when we are carrying high-interest debt (credit cards, car loans, etc.), each new expense we charge to those cards is costing us more dollar-for-dollar, because the interest from the debt is constantly setting us back. Make every effort to pay off high-interest debt as a way to reduce the "monthly nut" and make each dollar go further.

That's it. The list is not long, but putting it all into practice does take some doing. The goal is not to take the fun out of our lives by imposing too much structure and discipline. What we really want is to incorporate this thinking into our lives so that we can make good decisions from day to day. If we do that, we might be spared a harsh day of financial reckoning. The bill for the fun always comes due. But we can anticipate this bill by living smart.

If we use these principles to strengthen our "Business of One," developing new income sources and plugging expense leaks, we'll be less dependent on our jobs. Hopefully we'll be firing our employers sooner rather than later. Then we can choose work that is not only more lucrative, but more meaningful.

There's more than one way to free yourself from pink slip culture, but financial competence is at the heart of all of them.

Part VIII:

Conclusion: Success Beyond the Numbers

Overcoming Adversity

The Myth of Success and Failure (and the Feedback Loop)

Leaping Is a Fact of Life – The Concept of Lag

The Pursuit of Freedom Goes Beyond "9 to 5"

So You've Read the Book – Now What's Next?

"There's nothing more discouraging than realizing you are spending more money than you are making. And there's no worse feeling than knowing you are contributing to your own predicament."

Overcoming Adversity

There's not a lot more to it; the hard part is seeing it through. I have a few more tactics and refinements to share, and then the book is finished. The rest is in the doing. Before we cover the final concepts, I should say a few words about the resistance we are sure to encounter along the way.

The tactics in this book would be more effective if we were automated work machines, grinding our way through. But that's anything but true. There's nothing harder than facing our own frailty. The disappointments of the "almosts" add up – plan-wrecking hurricanes are everywhere. People are crippled by medical bills, tied to jobs they can't stomach, too far in debt to think straight. Others have been through divorces as expensive as they were difficult. If those setbacks sound hauntingly familiar, you are not alone.

Times like that make you forget about big plans; it's bitter to lose so much of what you've worked for. That's when we tend to dig a bigger hole, caught in a cycle of debt, over-spending on anything that can make us feel better. There's nothing more discouraging than realizing you are spending more money than you are making. And there's no worse feeling than knowing you are contributing to your own predicament by spending money on a comforting escape because you're too demoralized to see a way forward.

Earlier, I wrote that I respected financial competence because it cannot be achieved without emotional mastery. But good fortune also plays a role. Even if we execute brilliantly, there's no guarantee our assets will generate income; there's no promise our hard-won career will continue to provide job security. A few months of unemployment can set us back years.

That's why it's so important to choose projects with a payoff beyond cash. When you run your business the right way, empowering people with skills they never had, you get some of that payoff. When you finish a book like this one, you get the thrill of all those laptop nights adding up.

When you rehab a house, you pick up some carpentry skills, not to mention the satisfaction of a job well done. *The best way to avoid bitterness is to pursue projects with soul.* Grabbing some happiness along the way is the best insurance against uncertain outcomes. To thicken the plot, soulful projects must ultimately be marketable enough to support us. That is a worthy challenge.

I wish this book could reduce the adversity. Unfortunately, chasing a vision tends to bring on more difficulty. There may be something beautiful on the other side, but getting there is no picnic. Our fate is not determined by adversity, but it *is* defined by how we respond to it. The people I admire most have found ways of minimizing the impact of setbacks. And there are tactics we can borrow from them.

The first tactic is not to "pile on." When we take a hit, it's tempting to wallow, and the good money soon follows the bad. I call this "piling on," and the scene after a good session of piling on is a mess of pizza boxes and bad decisions. A gambling spree on an Indian reservation is one scenario you see around here, but there are countless others. Questionable choices are just one Internet connection away. The hardest thing is to drink the vinegar of our disappointment and stay the course.

Learning how not to pile on takes skill and resolve. Of course, comfort is not always bad. Scarfing down a pint of Ben and Jerry's after a rough day doesn't do much harm, but the pints tend to add up. Avoiding the "pile on" means reckoning with yourself and developing coping tactics. That process can take years. But it's important: excelling in one aspect of your life only to leak your progress out the other is not a good time. Just becoming aware of the dynamic can help. It's a great day when we endure a tough setback without taking it out on ourselves or losing faith in our potential.

The second technique is the famous cliché: "never give up," though I prefer the boxing version, "always pick yourself up off the mat." But I'd add a caveat that many personal growth cheerleaders overlook: dissect your performance first. Heading back into the ring with the same old stance is a good way to get knocked out. Before you go back into the fray, identify the weakness in your approach and adjust.

This is happening to me now. I'm making money and my business is stable, but I'm frustrated with the amount of sweat required. I need to develop income streams that require less effort. I might feel foolishly productive, but the joke will be on me next time I look up from my laptop and another decade has gone by. So I must pursue ventures with a better time/money exchange. I'm making some changes to that now based on the exposed weaknesses in my current strategy.

"Finding your passion," as some would have us do, is not going to cut it either. Passion honed with strategy is the key. It's the integration of theory and practice that allows you to change your circumstances. Analyze your disappointments, identify your skills gaps, and fill them. Then you'll be on the mat less often.

This "keep on fighting" talk implies that it all comes down to self-reliance. It's really the opposite: our accomplishments are largely due to the right relationships. This applies well beyond business. It's easy to fall under the illusion that strength is a matter of resolve and that leaning on others is a sign of weakness. Not true. Learning how to let people carry you is one of the greatest skills you can develop. Adversity humbles us, but it's our loneliness in the face of those setbacks that is devastating. It seems like people with strong bonds can face anything.

The final technique for overcoming adversity is to live for more than one thing. For many of us, this means cultivating a spiritual life, an understanding that we need to go within for inspiration instead of deriving our self-worth from the workplace. It's great to have professional focus, but the lack of balance undermines us. There's nothing more tiresome than the co-worker who lives to work, jockeying for position on every project. Having a life beyond work may seem obvious, but the ambitious people I know struggle with this, so it must not be so easy. It's certainly not easy for me.

The idea that we live in a "meritocracy" where success and hard work are inevitably rewarded is ludicrous. Success at the highest level involves luck and market momentum, two factors well beyond our control. No one has any business taking credit for all that, though some have the arrogance to do so.

The line between "success" and "failure" is one thin mofo, and don't let Donald Trump tell you different. Dreaming it doesn't necessarily mean you can do it, and no karmic law ensures that good people always get what they deserve. But the best dreams don't need to come true; their pursuit is its own reward. If that's not the case, then you're chasing the wrong dream. No matter how much adversity we encounter, pursuing the right dream is the path of no regrets.

"The fear of success is real, as it should be. Success comes with a price."

The Myth of Success and Failure (and the Feedback Loop)

We are limited by success and failure. Boxed in by perfectionism, the fear of failure haunts us. Less well advertised is the fear of success. But Nelson Mandela was right: what we fear most is our own potential.

What appears to be a "failure" rarely is. Most failures are useful feedback loops, carrying valuable information about what we are good at and what we are not. When we develop a comfort level with that loop, not getting too down when the phone stops ringing and not getting too high when somebody kisses our behind, then we can move into a continual state of improvement.

The end result? We stop taking the world so personally. Ironically, it's the freedom from approval that results in superior work. Those who are comfortable out on that limb, unconcerned with conventional success, have a strangely better chance of finding it. The system is far from perfect, but the material world does tend to reward people who have become exceptional. And you become that way through a very unromantic and non-magical process called trial and error.

Dig into the biographies: most people worth admiring confronted failure early and often. The sports world is filled with "cut from the team" stories. As a freshman, Michael Jordan was cut from his high school basketball team. Tom Brady was drafted in the sixth round. So many great champions made their run after a worthy foe exposed their weaknesses.

Many who fear failure are very "successful" by professional standards. *But they are not successful at the thing they love the most.* The guitar is still in the closet. The "someday" business never got further than a half-finished business plan which now sits under a houseplant. As mortgages kick in, we become competent at careers like office management or software sales. We cling to those competencies like life rafts. But when it comes time to taking a chance on something we always wanted, we hesitate. Suddenly there's a LOT more at stake. Sometimes it's better to be a legend in our own minds than to be exposed as mediocre.

I have friends who are writing legends, but *only* in their own minds. They waited too long to start the feedback loop; now they are afraid to begin. Daunted by the brilliance of their favorite books, they can't go further than a blank computer screen. The older you get, the more painful that empty screen becomes.

I spent so many years afraid to start writing that I almost didn't start at all. So we find other projects to obsess about, like the crabgrass problem in our backyards. Fill our lives with enough clutter, and we are reassured: "I don't have time to write a book." Isn't that better than finally making the time to do it, only to write a bad one?

What we forget is that being "bad" is part of becoming good. Legend has it that Stephen King tossed his first book in the trash – yet another example of why we must focus on meeting our own standards first. The critics and the doubters will kick and scream either way. The more you succeed, the louder they tend to holler. The solution? Keep improving.

The fear of success is an even more baffling phenomenon. When I bring it up, the barstool response is: "Fear of success?

What are you talking about?" But the fear of success is real, as well it should be. Success comes with a price.

Before we can go after the big dreams, we have to cut loose all the "friends" who had a stake in our ongoing misery. They'd never admit it, but our stagnation has been a comfort to them. So you have to leave the wing clippers behind.

It may be freeing to take the leap, but there are reasons to fear success. Even when change is for the best, there is a sadness to the process. It's hard to cut the old gang loose, but more often than not, stepping into our own potential means doing just that.

But our problematic friends are nothing compared to ourselves. Living audaciously means junking comfortable habits. A night of drinking with our peeps is a lot more appealing than a night in the lab, working on ventures that highlight all our shortcomings. Being the best we can be is hard work. More often than not, we are our own worst enemies. We fear success because of how much it demands of us. If we are capable of so much, then why do we settle for so little?

It's not easy to face the ways we held ourselves back. In college, I turned my back on a writing career, playing it safe with a pre-law curriculum instead. Trying to reclaim this career in mid-life is taking everything I can muster. I can feel sorry for myself all I want, but that is the price of my particular ticket.

I hope this book can make a difference in two ways: by inspiring people to act, and by giving them a "game plan." Too often, we're naively encouraged to chase our dreams but not provided with a strategy that takes into account what we're up against. Hopefully, concepts like the feedback loop will convince some folks to give it another shot: armed with a better strategy, we should have a better outcome. And in terms of tactics, there's nothing in this book more valuable than using the feedback loop to move beyond perfectionism.

The marketplace provides invaluable feedback each time we enter it. But the big reward of the feedback loop is psychological. Eventually, you get into a groove. You get used to putting your work out there. While you are curious about what people think, you are no longer defined by it. On a certain level, you just don't care anymore. Not because the feedback isn't useful – it is. You don't care because you are free from the paralysis of attaching your self-worth to a project. You understand that success is a process, and the process happens by putting work out there, even when it's flawed.

In Zen terms, you embrace the "beginner's mind" and learn to love the learning curve. The more at peace you are with your own awkwardness, the more you can learn. (At least that's what I tell myself each week at my "back to square one" guitar lessons.)

The feedback loop is the market's way of letting you know which ideas resonate. What we hear back is not always what we wanted to hear, but we ignore the loop at our peril. To this day, the most common emails I receive are from SAP consultants looking for career advice. I would prefer that my writing on unsung 80s metal gods was what people responded to most, but it just hasn't happened. My music journalism is the best writing I have ever done, but the feedback loop has been clear: the market values my SAP writing more.

That feedback can be a horse pill, but it is invaluable. So what do I do with that information? Does it mean I stop writing about unsung hair bands? Nope – couldn't if I tried. But if I think a hair band book is going to put me on a yacht, I am pretty naïve.

So, I will continue to use my SAP knowledge, which the feedback loop has certified as marketable, to finance other projects. I'll keep doing the hair band tributes, but not too often. The more money you have in the bank, the more you can err on the side of your own interests. But I'm at a point where I still need to find a middle ground between my passions and what the market will pay me for. This book is another experiment along those lines. I'm not sure what the feedback loop will prove.

Be ready for curveballs! One shocking development is how much I truly enjoy my SAP work these days. In large part, this is due to being honored as an SAP Mentor and being asked to play a bigger role in SAP's online communities, where I am energized by working with many brilliant and creative personalities who continually raise the bar. Just because you go where the marketplace beckons doesn't mean you can't add some individuality to the equation. In fact, I'd encourage you to do just that. Sometimes we tone ourselves down for corporate work way more than we need to. As we go to press, I'm planning to launch a more experimental SAP podcast series – thus furthering my fascination with the podcasting format, stoking some old fires about being a DJ, and upping the ante in terms of stamping the SAP field with more of my own personality. So I'm flying my freak flag higher, but I'm still paying attention to the expectations of that particular market.

Some might argue that you should ignore the marketplace because "money can't buy happiness anyway." They may be correct, but only to a point. Studies on happiness have shown that beyond survival, money has a diminishing return, becoming less important than community, family, and romantic love. But money is still a big part of happiness; it reduces our dependence on amoral institutions beyond our direct control.

In a market economy, money defines the terms of engagement. Money allows us to finance ambition and send a few kids to school. "Life on our own terms" might be at the heart of the working definitions for both success and happiness. So there *is* a connection between success, happiness, and finance. The exact formula is different for everyone, but in a market economy, removing finance from the equation is philosophically questionable.

There is also something to be said for mastering your craft. That kind of expertise tends to lead to whatever people call "success." Money is usually a happy byproduct of that process. By the time we've mastered our craft, we should be able to live off of it. If not, then we probably ignored the feedback loop. That's OK, we can still make changes – if not to our focus, then to how it is marketed.

You can often redefine your area of mastery to make it more marketable without giving up the essence of the project. Real-life Example 1: you are a photographer who prefers doing your own exhibits. You start doing some weddings on the side to pay the bills until your exhibit work starts to sell. Real-life Example 2: you run a popular Web site. You decide to keep the content free but to place advertisements on it. You might prefer to go ad-free, but this gives you a better chance of funding your life. Strike your own balance.

A truly successful person is someone who has rejected success and failure in favor of an ongoing process of mastery. If you can do that while being good to those around you, you're already one of life's rock stars. By the time others start calling you successful, it won't even matter anymore. If making it big is overrated, then it's time to glamorize the humble process of becoming the best person you can be, beyond success and failure.

"When you cash an IRA to invest in a startup, you'll feel the breeze. When you downshift to part-time in order to pursue a side venture, you'll feel it too. Be prepared for those cash flow hits. Some will hurt; some will pay off in a big way."

Leaping Is a Fact of Life – The Concept of Lag

We all want to live at a high level, but few are willing to leap. And leaping is non-negotiable. The right tactics minimize risk, but we're always going to feel the breeze.

If we wait until our next move is assured, years will sneak by. Waiting for the right time is how people become ordinary. Developing a practice of habitual, calculated risk is the smartest response to the failed guarantees of the 9 to 5 lifestyle. The ultimate definition of entrepreneurialism is having the confidence to create new (and better) structures rather than accepting those imposed upon us by amoral institutions.

Those with a spiritual bent would call this type of creation an act of faith – an acknowledgement that to live as the gods intended us to live, we have to take that huge first step without knowing what lies ahead. More often than not, those who take that leap find that something meets them halfway. Thoreau used to say that when you take that leap, kinder laws of the universe go into affect and carry you forward. But that's not always the case: there is also such a thing as a hard landing.

So what happens when we make our move only to smack into a wall? Success guru Tony Robbins used to talk about the concept of lag. "Lag" provides one explanation for the phenomenon of delayed transformation. Lag dictates that there will be a delay between any change we make to our lives and the definitive signs that the change is working. Unfortunately, the reality of lag opens us up to all kinds of self-sabotage.

Most fail not because they didn't try, but because they gave up before a better way took hold. Lag is a beast to endure. True, some changes do happen quickly, like telling your boss to find someone else to exploit or reconciling with an ex. But most changes take significant time, and while the change plays out behind the scenes, there's plenty of opportunity to second-guess, and second-guessing often leads to self-sabotage.

Lag is humbling. How many of us have unfinished projects we abandoned when we ran out of steam? I have a half-written screenplay about zombies that broke my will easily. Now it sits there unfinished, mocking me and my desire to write screenplays. We all have friends enduring difficult stages in their careers, toughing it out in statistics classes while working full time, or busting tail at restaurants while trying to pull together the right prerequisites for medical school.

Financial changes are like that too. We resolve to get out of debt finally and for good, and then we get hammered by an expensive emergency room visit and lose faith in our plan. There are all kinds of ways to lose momentum. Even the best dreams feel like a grind sometimes. And it's hard to keep grinding when you have waning faith that you will ever arrive.

Be forewarned: implementing the tactics in this book may set you back financially before you move ahead. When you look at success in business, you always have an investment cycle – a period where you have to sink money into new products or to enhance your competitive position.

When you cash an IRA to invest in a startup, you'll feel the breeze. When you downshift to part-time in order to pursue a side venture, you'll feel it too. Be prepared for those cash flow hits. Some will hurt; some will pay off in a big way.

That's not how most of us were raised. My family saw finances as scrimping and saving, stashing nuts in the tree. This book is not about stashing nuts. This book is about how corporate America can smash our nut collection with the ease of a pink slip. Fortunately, there is a response. But it means putting that nut stash in play and believing we can always find more. Building a better life is a beautiful project, but it's not an easy one. If it was, more people would be doing it.

So we're back to where we started. We've got tactics that *do* work but require sacrifices along the way. So why bother with the hard road? Why suffer the nights in the lab, especially if money never mattered that much in the first place? Well, some of us do it because we're hopelessly infected with the entrepreneurial bug. We're certified whack jobs.

Used to be, the rest of us could just focus on our careers and our families. This book argues that our hands are now being forced. The instability of 9 to 5 work has upped the ante. The institutions that once offered a paycheck in exchange for loyalty have changed the premise.

But we don't have to take the raw end of that deal lying down. I've seen people raise themselves out of some pretty daunting muck. Most of them had to endure that self-doubting "lag period" and stay the course before their dream came to fruition.

Along the way, we will be tested. We'll do great work that goes unnoticed; we'll invest in projects that fail; we'll get burned by those we trusted. But we'll learn. And over time, we'll build a stronger future than the one advertised to us in the guise of a so-called corporate "career."

"Living 'Free From Corporate America' means a strength of body and spirit. We might still work with (and for) large companies. But we know our financial security comes from our own skills and imagination."

The Pursuit of Freedom Goes Beyond 9 to 5

They say that 1/4 of all Americans are already "freelancers," but how many of us are really free? Even the definition of freedom is open to question. The pursuit of "financial freedom" is one way to change our destiny, but the all-out pursuit of any goal can prove to be its undoing. We all know people who achieved their financial objectives but ended up with a big list of regrets.

When I think back to my 9 to 5 years, I can't help but question them. Most folks who work behind a desk for ten years start to resemble the furniture they sit in. We ante up bodies and sometimes souls for employers that don't return the favor. That's why the focus of this book has been achieving financial autonomy. With better control over when and how we work, the rest of our lives balance out accordingly.

If financial autonomy is so important, then why are some of the happiest people mired in money problems? For one thing, this book is not about happiness, it's about freedom, and the two are not the same. But the overlap is still instructive: the happiest people I know have a combination of meaningful work and inspired relationships.

It's harder to find happiness when you're scrapping for rent, but I know people I'd consider happy who are in just that circumstance. They have one thing in common: they haven't signed over to all-consuming work. They may not have money, but they've fought for their time. Their time is the wild card in their hand, which they use on their kids, their show dogs, or their garden. They've found a place in their lives that the demands of work can't touch.

So does that invalidate my premise? If so many keys to happiness lie outside of work and money, then why fight that particular fight?

Because the terms of employment have changed. We can't take careers for granted, even as a means of basic subsistence. And without subsistence, happiness is hard to come by. But money doesn't just provide a safety net. It buys time, and it also buys opportunities.

Excess cash can be powerfully applied. I've dreamed about creating funds for aspiring artists, building wildlife sanctuaries, financing independent films. It's not really about the skills anymore. Money is now the major obstacle in my way.

But having said that, the biggest payoffs from following this process are not financial. Most corporate workhorses I know are just that – overworked and overstressed, overweight and over-traveled.

Living "Free From Corporate America" means a strength of body and spirit. We might still work with (and for) large companies, but we know our financial security comes from our own skills and imagination. We create new opportunities to replace anything we lose. We are now able to walk away if the terms of engagement ask too much in exchange for too little.

That kind of "walk away confidence" doesn't come easily. That's why I wrote this book. Not just to bolster the confidence of readers, but to bolster my own. There is work ahead: I'll be taking my own advice and focusing on screenplays, with the intention of breaking into film production. These are the assets I hope to create next. If I can pull it off, maybe I'll be able to strike a balance between work that engages me and work that has market value.

If I can achieve that, perhaps I will finally find a version of "success" that suits me. While I was finishing this book, I stumbled on an essay about this from Maria Shriver. What she said was that the best kind of success emanates from our own power. That power takes longer to claim because it must be an external manifestation of whatever unique qualities we have – qualities that must be cultivated and then realized in the outside world. That's not easy to find through a cookie cutter career.

There are two reasons I believe in this book. One is the importance of cultivating attitude. Work of all kinds, especially corporate work, can beat the attitude right out of us. By attitude, I'm not talking about "she has a great attitude about staying late and filing all those expense reports." I'm talking about what performance artist Megan E. LaBonte calls "Sass" – a natural exuberance that we can take on the world without settling for less. Most of us had plenty of that when we were young, but few have aged well in that regard. Whatever we have to do to get that fierceness back is worth it. Living with more attitude (and less fear) is what *Free From Corporate America* is all about.

It may seem strange that I wrote so much about money while at the same time conceding its limitations. It's true that a narrow pursuit of success is a trap. But I think back to that under-appreciated concept from *Jerry Maguire*, that achievement/state of mind known as "Kwan." Kwan, as Jerry's only client Rod Tidwell memorably explained to him, is way more than just getting paid.

In the context of Kwan, money is the manifestation of excellence, the indicator of a person in harmony with their relationships, their talent and their self-respect. Kwan is about being paid what you are worth without undue compromise. The pursuit of Kwan in a world of job insecurity is, without a doubt, a daring act. But I can't think of anything better to shoot for.

And that's the other reason I wrote this book: I don't believe most corporate careers offer a chance to achieve Kwan. The personal sacrifices are too great, the financial payoffs too minimal. There has never been a better opportunity to re-invent our work lives through the entrepreneurial economy. But to pull it off, we need more than attitude – we need a method.

I have not arrived at my dreamiest goals, but the ideas in this book have already changed my life. It's been a privilege to apply them to the problem so many of us face: forging a better life in circumstances that can seem daunting.

The presence of a global labor pool will continue to encourage a "use and discard" approach to hiring – an approach that will be attractive to shareholders. It might be great news for the corporate bottom line, but it's not such good news for folks who count on job security.

I wrote this book during the most difficult years of my adult life. But I found a way to get these chapters done because I needed to believe some dreams were not beyond my reach. There is a way to be compensated for our best work. One of our biggest jobs in life is to find it.

Along the way, perhaps we can create a new approach to work – sometimes working for larger companies, sometimes pursuing our own ventures – but always with a tactical plan that ensures we will end up owning assets instead of being owned.

Employment is a use-use proposition. I've spent too many years being juiced by companies all too willing to squeeze. And yet I put up with it, mostly because I had no plan as strong as my fears. But life rewards initiative, not complacency. This book has given me a roadmap, a place to turn to when I lose my professional bearings. If it does the same for a few others, then the endeavor has been worth it.

"I can't claim to be Nostradamus; it didn't take a genius to decide that stocks were overvalued, the market was careless and greedy, that corporations would hire and fire with impunity, and that we put too much faith in home ownership, in particular the notion that property values would always rise."

So You've Read the Book – Now What's Next?

Now that you've read the book, the real fun (and real work) begins: applying the ideas in this book to your own life, in your own way. This book was supposed to be different: instead of selling you a "one-size-fits-all" way of life, I tried to share an approach that you can slice and dice to create your own strategy.

I knew I was writing about a moving target. The FreeFromCorporateAmerica.com Web site is intended to help by providing important updates. I also hope it will also serve as a forum to continue the conversation, giving readers like you a chance to pose follow up questions to me directly. You can post comments at the end of any of the online chapters.

This book is a bit unusual; it pulls from both business and philosophy books I scoured over a fifteen year period. At first, I struggled with how to properly recognize my sources without turning the book into an academic exercise, bogged down in footnotes. I realized the Web site would serve as a great way to give my sources their due while linking to online discussions about their ideas.

So, in the "Resources" section of FreeFromCorporateAmerica.com, you can read more about this book's biggest influences. Some of my references, such as Robert Kiyosaki's *Rich Dad* series and *Your Money or Your Life*, are probably obvious. But you might find my opinions about the pros and cons of these books worth a read.

In the "Resources" section, you will also find links to more data about the reality of white collar globalization. In this book, I take it for granted that the globalization of the information worker is an unfolding reality that deserves a serious response. I didn't waste space debating a point I think is already proven, but online, I have linked to a number of resources and discussion forums where a healthy discussion over the extent of globalization and its positive (or not-so-positive) impact is now taking place.

But the Web site serves as more than a resources section. I have now posted podcast introductions to some of the most important chapters that will give you more context for how I approached them. My first-ever radio interview on the book is here as well. If you check the "FFCA Podcasts" section, you can also hear new podcast interviews on getting the most out of your online ventures. I have also published new material, some of which is designed to flesh out this book's tactics when it comes to topics such as print-on-demand publishing and keys to marketing your work online. Most of that material can be subscribed to via RSS feeds as well.

In the "Bonus Book Material" section, you will find fresh information I did not include in this book. One of the highlights: a new chapter on "Obstacles to Getting Started" that takes a hard look at some of the criticisms I have received on the book so far.

Since I began this book in 2005, there are two trends that deserve more attention than I gave in the book itself. One is the rise of social media sites such as Facebook, MySpace, LinkedIn and Twitter. We need to understand how these sites can help (or hurt) us as we pursue the strategies in this book. I am planning a Web site chapter on "Building Your Marketing Platform and the Dangers of Social Media" that you will be able to read online.

The other key development is alluded to in the first pages of this book: as we head towards publication, the economy is now in a tailspin that has raised valid questions about the usefulness of my approach in a downturn. To address this, I have already posted a chapter online entitled "How Does *Free From Corporate America* Apply to a Down Economy?"

I hope you will find the entire chapter interesting, but here are a couple of excerpts. First, on how my book seems to anticipate the crummy things that have happened:

"I can't claim to be Nostradamus; it didn't take a genius to decide that stocks were overvalued, the market was careless and greedy, that corporations would hire and fire with impunity, and that we put too much faith in home ownership, in particular the notion that property values would always rise. It was good to see some accountability return to the market, but on the other hand, a lot of people have suffered as a result. None of it changed my resolve to get this book in print."

And in terms of my book's relevance to our current predicament:

"I've been thinking a lot about this, trying to mentally summon a crystal ball, and the only thing I have for you right now is not something very reassuring: everything is harder than it was before the markets crashed. That's it. Furthering your career is harder, saving money is harder, putting the principles of this book into action is harder. That's not chicken soup, but it is what it is."

I go on to talk about how innovation can occur in a downturn, and how we can be on the lookout for certain kinds of opportunities in the circumstances we now face. At some point, the economy will shift again, but since I do not expect globalization to go away, the tactics in this book will remain relevant. Yes, the villains of the day may change – swap Ken Lay for

Bernie Madoff, or AIG for WorldCom – but the message is the same: excessive dependence on amoral institutions is not the way forward. Especially when the opportunity for something better is waiting for us to seize it, if we can stop clinging to things that aren't stable in the first place.

That's probably the best place to end on, reckoning with our fears on the one hand, and dreaming of a better way on the other. Perhaps the way forward is a bit easier with the tactics in this book to guide us. It's good to remember that survival is not all we are challenged to do. Yes, some of us are now fighting just to hold on. But we can keep our grip on the present without short selling our future. Regardless of who you voted for in the last election, it was a stunning reminder that not all outcomes are scripted. We won't get everything we set out for, but there is a necessary dignity that can only be found when we dare to aspire. So gather your plans, take a chance on your talents, and head straight towards the improbable. I hope I meet you somewhere on that brash and unforgettable journey.

With that, I wish you all the best in your endeavors and look forward to continuing this conversation online.

Jon Reed
Northampton, Massachusetts
FreeFromCorporateAmerica.com

About the Author

Jon Reed has been involved in entrepreneurial business since the early '90s. He currently runs his own publishing and consulting company. Jon is twisted enough to consider writing books a hobby - *Free From Corporate America* is Jon's third book. His second book, *Resumes From Hell*, has its own web site, **ResumesFromHell.com**

Jon is currently the President of **JonERP.com**, a web site dedicated to helping SAP professionals make sense of SAP's technical evolution.

Jon is also a founding board member of **Hidden-Tech.net**, a regional organization that serves as an advocacy and networking group for a growing base of "virtual companies."

Jon has a passion for helping people to develop a more entrepreneurial approach to their careers. He believes that the "corporate contract" has been broken, and that it's time for people to regain economic control of their lives.

Free From Corporate America shares some of Jon's favorite tactics and business philosophies, a conversation which continues on **FreeFromCorporateAmerica.com**. Those who want to delve deeper into Jon's obsessions are invited to check out **JonReed.net**, Jon's "essays, rants, and more" web site. •

Free From Corporate America – Book Index

(key concepts, memorable phrases, and a few celebrities)

A

B

C

D

E

F

G

H

I

J

K

L

M

N

O

P

R

S

T

V

W

Also by Jon Reed

The SAP Consultant Handbook
(samples available on JonERP.com)

Resumes From Hell
(samples available on ResumesFromHell.com)

About *Resumes From Hell:*

Some resumes are good, some are bad, and some are simply from Hell. The all-too-real resumes in this book were no doubt written with the best of intentions, but a job search can be a misadventure. A wacky resume is a sure-fire way to derail your job application and slip from the interview pile into the "joke file." In this illustrated "how not to," former recruiters Jon Reed and Rachel Meyers open up their own joke files, and share highlights from the worst (and funniest) resumes they ever received. From "Questionable References" to "Hostile Email Interactions," Jon and Rachel take the reader through more resume mishaps and job search meltdowns than they ever knew existed, sneaking in a bit of job search wisdom on the fly. The resumes in this book have been changed to protect the not-so-innocent, but *Resumes From Hell* is proof that truth is still stranger – and funnier – than fiction.

You Can Have an Impact On This Book's Success

I have no idea if this book will strike a chord with anyone besides myself. I only know that I was determined to make any sacrifice necessary to finish it. If you're someone who was affected by this book, I want you to know that you can make a big difference on whether this book gets into the hands of the right readers.

I made some fateful decisions during the writing process that now challenge my ability to market this book as broadly as it deserves. I don't regret those decisions. I wanted this book to have an edge of realism not often found in "happy talk" business titles like *The 4 Hour Workweek* and its many rose-colored predecessors. I have a much more jaded eye towards the flaws of big business when it comes to looking out for individuals like you and me. Bottom line: I knew this book would require total editorial freedom to live up to its potential.

The marketing challenge boils down to this: *without passionate word of mouth support, this book is not going to be successful.* I have priced this book to be affordable. If you are inspired to share your copy with friends, or even buy extras on Amazon and give them to those who might benefit, it would mean something to me. A thoughtful review on Amazon is a huge help as well. Buying copies on Amazon is a big factor because each copy purchased will raise the book's profile in Amazon's system.

I'm not someone who typically asks for help, but in this case, I will only succeed if like-minded readers go the extra mile. Thanks for reading this far, and I hope you'll be my partner in subversion as we push these ideas to the front of a discussion that is too often limited by small minds and status quo tendencies.. – JR –

Free From Corporate America – Jot Your Thoughts Here

Free From Corporate America – Jot Your Thoughts Here

www.ingramcontent.com/pod-product-compliance
Lightning Source LLC
LaVergne TN
LVHW090936080826
845145LV00003B/767

* 9 7 8 0 9 7 2 5 9 8 8 5 9 *